Breaking into Film

making your career search a blockbuster

Kenna McHugh

Peterson's
Princeton, New Jersey

About Peterson's

Peterson's is the country's largest educational information/communications company, providing the academic, consumer, and professional communities with books, software, and online services in support of lifelong education access and career choice. Well-known references include Peterson's annual guides to private schools, summer programs, colleges and universities, graduate and professional programs, financial aid, international study, adult learning, and career guidance. Peterson's Web site at petersons.com is the only comprehensive—and most heavily traveled—education resource on the Internet. The site carries all of Peterson's fully searchable major databases and includes financial aid sources, test-prep help, job postings, direct inquiry and application features, and specially created Virtual Campuses for every accredited academic institution and summer program in the U.S. and Canada that offers in-depth narratives, announcements, and multimedia features.

Visit Peterson's Education Center on the Internet (World Wide Web) at www.petersons.com

Copyright © 1999 by Peterson's

Library of Congress Cataloging-in-Publication data

McHugh, Kenna.
    Breaking into film : making your career search a blockbuster / Kenna McHugh.
        p.   cm.
    Includes index.
    ISBN 0-7689-0123-5
    1. Motion pictures—Vocational guidance. I. Title.
PN1995.9.P75M37   1998
791.43′02′93—dc21   98-33228
                                                                          CIP

Printed in the United States of America

10   9   8   7   6   5   4   3   2   1

contents

introduction

Why try to break into film as a "behind-the-scenes" professional? Because the industry is experiencing dramatic growth. The film and video industry is a significant employer, both in California and other parts of the country, of professionals in any number of fields.

Recently, the American Film Marketing Association (AFMA) launched a study on the economic impact filmmakers have on the economy as a whole. Its findings are exciting ones for those eager to work in the entertainment industry—and particularly for people interested in work that does not involve the financial (and emotional) risks associated with such fields as acting and screenwriting. AFMA's study paints a picture of a mature and growing industry in need of qualified professionals in a wide variety of disciplines.

- Filmmakers—both independents and major studios—account for more than 408,000 "direct" jobs nationwide. (This excludes people who work as consultants or freelancers.)

- The film industry's "total U.S. economic effect" is estimated at nearly $12.5 billion.

- Total production costs of network prime-time television, first-run syndication programs, and cable and pay-TV offerings are estimated at $12.8 billion.

The study closes by acknowledging the "growing demand for content in the entertainment industry" and the "many new formats and opportunities provided by emerging telecommunications and computer technologies." The industry is, in short, growing fast and likely to continue to do so.

As though to underscore AFMA's research, current news stories have pointed to continued strong growth in the entertainment sector. Among the most interesting recent signs of expansion:

- In 1996, Disney reported a quarterly earnings increase of 22 percent.
- Moviefone—the ubiquitous media company that provides movie listings for 12,000 movie screens in 30 cities nationwide, and advance ticket sales by phone—just reported a quarterly earnings increase of 16 percent.

To be sure, such figures rise and fall, and business shifts can come upon even large and successful companies with very little warning. As of this writing, however, the production of filmed entertainment clearly represents a major domestic economic success—and a huge export to international markets. If you're interested in learning about the most creative, effective ways of entering "the business" for the first time, this book will show you how. You'll learn:

- Why the film industry is exploding
- What kinds of jobs there are in the industry
- How to write effective resumes and letters
- The basics of networking
- How to make the most of your existing experience
- How to get the experience you need
- How to ace the interview (formal or informal)
- Who the major (and not-so-major) employers are

. . . and much more.

If you're ready to take the step of moving into a career in the film industry . . . read on!

chapter 1

The Entertainment Explosion

Just about everyone loves going to the movies, just like you. If you didn't, you wouldn't be reading this book. Just walking into a movie theater, buying your ticket, and finding a seat in the dimly lit auditorium excites you. And once the house lights go out and the celluloid shadows begin moving across the screen, you leave your own world behind and enter a new, different, and exciting one. It's magic.

And you're certainly not alone. Both in the United States and all over the world, going to the movies is one of the most popular forms of entertainment. In fact, according to the latest industry statistics, movies are attended by people in the United States close to 1.3 billion times every year, bringing $6.5 billion in annual revenues.

Like you, most of those moviegoers recognize the actors starring in the films—it is, after all, one of the reasons they go—and many are familiar with previous works by the directors. But chances are you've probably never heard of most of the people who work behind the scenes, the ones who make those movies come alive. The fact is, though, that there are hundreds of hardworking, talented, and creative people behind every star in a film. These people include set painters, electricians, sound recordists, makeup artists, film editors, publicists, location scouts, casting directors, animators, and more. And finding a job in one of these exciting fields in the film industry is exactly what this book is about.

THE FILM INDUSTRY EXPLOSION

The movies are not only one of the most popular forms of entertainment, they also represent an industry that's growing every year and, in that growth, creating thousands of job opportunities.

Hollywood produces and/or distributes between 400 and 500 films every year. That's more than a film a day. It is growing rapidly because, according to *Career Guide to America's Top Industries*, many of the billions of dollars Americans spend every year to be entertained are spent in the film industry. In addition, the increased availability of cable and satellite television has spurred demand for film and videotape production of domestic and foreign television, home video, and informational, educational, and industrial films. In response to this demand, employment in motion picture production and distribution is projected to increase 33 percent over the ten-year period between 1996 and 2006, more than twice the 14 percent growth projected for all industries combined.

New technology also continues to offer opportunities for the entertainment industry. As growth in the videocassette and cable television markets has slowed, satellite broadcasting and the Internet have come forward as likely new delivery systems for entertainment programming. These advances in technology should contribute to the success, even dominance, of the U.S. entertainment industry.

Moreover, Hollywood films are by no means limited to distribution in the United States. American films are shown all over the world, and the international marketplace has for many years been an integral part of the success of the United States entertainment industry. The Motion Picture Association of America (MPAA) reported that in 1995 its member companies, the major filmmakers, earned nearly 42 percent of their revenues from foreign markets, up from 34 percent in 1988.

What does all this growth mean? It means more employment opportunities in the film industry across the board. There will, of course, be an increase in the glamorous, higher-pay jobs for actors, directors, cinematographers, screenwriters, and producers, although comparatively few will find regular work in these areas because competition is fierce. More important, there will be thousands of opportunities for lower-paying, less glamorous, but nevertheless exciting, behind-the-scenes jobs such as production assistants, grips, set construction workers, and others. There is also expected to be considerable job growth in film reproduction and distribution, as more large studios turn to this part of the business in response to the demand for more products on cable and for video rentals. These entry-level positions are the first steps toward more responsible and higher-paying jobs.

There has, in short, never been a better time to seek a career in film and television. In California, the heart of the industry, according to the recent *MPAA State of The Industry—The Economic Impact of the Entertainment Industry on California—Report*, from 1992 to 1996 entertainment production—the manufacture of motion pictures, commercials, and television programs—was the star of California's economic recovery. In 1996 alone, the industry generated $27.5 billion in economic activity statewide. Over this four-year period, total employment in the industry rose from 164,000 to 226,000, a 38 percent increase—seven times faster than any other major sector in the state.

By the end of 1996, the industry was larger than California's insurance, real estate, industrial machinery, transportation equipment, computer and office equipment, auto repair and parking, auto dealer and service, and legal services and communications industries and comparable with the state's mammoth electronic equipment sector. The report also points out that entertainment production was a substantial factor in leading California out of recession, and that it remains one of the state's most vital industrial resources. From 1992 to 1996, the industry generated some of the state's most rapid job growth and highest incomes.

If California is the heart of the film industry, New York might be said to be its brain, and the story on the East Coast is no different. CNNfn, the financial network, reported that in 1997, 213 movies and 105 television shows were at least partially shot in New York City, bringing $5 billion into the metropolitan area's economy. Julianne Cho, director of special events at the Mayor's Office of Film, Theatre and Broadcasting, stated in the report, "Right now the city is riding a stunning wave of production. We're in our fourth consecutive record-breaking year of production." In addition, according to the *New York Film Commission News*, direct expenditures for 1997 totaled $2.37 billion, compared to $2.23

billion the previous year. Film and television productions shot the equivalent of 21,339 days on location during 1997, the highest number ever.

As you can see from these figures, not only are there opportunities in the film industry, but those opportunities are increasing every day. So if you love the idea of working in films, and you're willing to work hard at it, there's a place in the industry for you.

WHAT AND WHERE THE JOBS ARE

Job opportunities in the film industry consist of both full-time and freelance positions. While there are advantages and disadvantages to both, one common denominator is that there are and will continue to be openings in both areas. But the two types of positions have other important things in common, and these lie within the realm of what it takes to be a success.

To start with, unlike many other industries, a college education is not a prerequisite for working in films. Creative talent is always more important than a college degree. Of course, some of the people hired by the studios are college graduates, but some haven't even finished high school. As one professional put it, "In this business you don't have to be educated in a formal school. You can learn the business by doing. If you follow the rules, you are a success in five years. This is the only business where you can make millions and have your name plastered all over the world without a college education. You just can't do that anywhere else."

Another common factor is that, whether full-time or freelance, you have to be ready to work long, hard hours—in the beginning, usually, for low pay—work whenever you're needed, and generally be willing and able to go that extra mile. If you're not, you might as well give up on the idea of working in the industry. It's as competitive a business as any on earth, and if you're not willing to pay the dues, there are lots of other people who are.

Getting into—and being a success in—the film industry requires a lot of hard work and persistence coupled with preparation and opportunity. It's very rare that a person is *handed* a job in any industry, let alone in as competitive an industry as films. You'll have to establish yourself as a person who can get along well with others while getting the job done, so a positive attitude is a must.

In the end, though, the most important similarities between freelance and full-time workers are their love of the business, their desire to contribute to the creation of the magic of movies, and to see the results of those contributions reflected on the screens of dimly lit movie houses all over the world.

Full-Time Positions

The great majority of the available full-time positions are with specialized suppliers and services directly related to the production industry, such as film labs, special effects and digital studios, locations services, prop and wardrobe houses, research services and film stock houses, videotape duplicating services, and stage rental facilities. These include such jobs as optical timer, model maker, storyboard artist, and production secretary. Salaries generally start at around $27,000, but experienced people in these fields can earn as much as $125,000 each year.

Aside from the general qualities mentioned above for both freelance and full-time workers, such positions usually require experienced candidates who are quick, organized, precise, have good ideas, and work well with others.

As in any industry, there are advantages and disadvantages to full-time employment. Probably the most important advantage is the knowledge that you'll receive a paycheck every week. Although no one is ever guaranteed employment (except Supreme Court justices, who are appointed for life), if you do a good job and avoid antagonizing anyone (particularly your boss), barring unforeseen circumstances, the chances are you won't have to worry about feeding yourself. In addition, as in other industries, full-time workers generally are entitled to a wide range of government-prescribed benefits, including paid vacations and holidays and health-care and retirement benefits.

On the other hand, there are disadvantages to such a position. For example, you have to worry about pleasing your boss, you have to go to work every day, and you usually have to do the same job, day in and day out. If, however, security is more important to you than anything else, a full-time position is the kind you should be looking for.

Freelance Positions

Virtually all the positions available in film production itself are freelance. Not only are the actors, directors, and other high-visibility workers hired on a temporary basis, so too are virtually all the behind-the-scenes people. Here you will find such jobs as gaffer, lamp operator, property manager, script supervisor, etc.

In addition to the general qualities mentioned above, the people who are most likely to get these sought-after freelance jobs are generally those who are organized, fairly extroverted, and good team players. It's the unit production managers who do the hiring for these jobs, and learning how to reach these people is discussed at length later in the book.

Among the advantages to freelance work are the opportunities to choose your own jobs (to the extent that you have a choice), to work when you want to (providing you can afford it), and to escape from the same day in, day out routine that you might otherwise have. In short, being a freelancer gives you a level of freedom that you can't have when you're committed to a full-time job.

There are, however, also disadvantages, the most obvious of which is that you're never quite sure where your next paycheck is coming from. It takes a certain type of person to live with that kind of uncertainty, and if you think it's likely to be a problem for you, it would be better for you to seek a full-time job.

Also, unlike individuals with full-time jobs, as a freelancer you're not entitled to any benefits. There are, however, guilds and unions that represent the vast majority of the freelance workforce in the film industry and take an active interest in the well-being of their members—and their members' families—that extends well beyond the confines of the workplace. The International Alliance of Theatrical Stage Employees, Moving Picture Technicians, Artists and Allied Crafts of the United States and Canada, AFL-CIO, CLC (IATSE) is the union that represents the largest percentage of people in behind-the-scenes jobs in the industry. Like other unions and guilds, IATSE not only represents its members to employers but also offers health, pension, and vacation plans.

Many of those working on low-budget productions are not union or guild members. Some jobs on low-budget productions offer "flats" to nonunion workers, which is $50 to $100 a day. A day is 24 hours long, which means essentially that people work until they're told to go home or until they drop from exhaustion.

Here is a typical scenario of someone—we'll call him Alex—starting out in the movie business on a freelance basis as a "go-fer" or a production assistant. Alex is generally paid less than union wages—on average between $50 and $100 per 16-hour day, six days a week. The pay is so poor, in fact, that some beginners work for free just to get known and to build up their resumes.

Once Alex establishes himself as a hard worker with a good attitude and the ability to work well with others, a production crew hires him permanently and gets him in the union. Now he's making $150 a day, plus overtime and penalty fees. (Penalty fees are how unions protect their members from anything production companies do that create inconveniences on the job. For example, after regular hours members must get overtime, which pays anywhere from time-and-a-half to double-time. And if a member works Sundays, it's called "golden time," because the $150 daily wage becomes the hourly wage.)

As a union member, Alex is also entitled to a whole array of perks, such as extra pay for using his vehicle on the set and extra pay if he's not allowed the standard 12-hour turn-around-time to report back to the set after a full day's work. By the time he adds up his regular hourly wage, overtime, and penalty fees, Alex can take home a nice healthy paycheck. A set painter, for example, recently reported that he averages $27,000 per picture on union wages. A production assistant working on location made over $1,300 a week.

Nonpaying Jobs

In addition to full-time and freelance jobs, there's actually a third way you can work in the film industry—for free. It probably doesn't sound like a very good idea and certainly not something you'd want—or be able—to do for too long, but it is a way to get a foot in the door.

There are, in fact, film productions where crews are "hired" for no pay at all. In such instances, the producer may offer the crew shares in the film or some other form of deferred payment—the chance to make money if and when the film itself makes money. If nothing else, the opportunity to share in the profits of the film should serve as considerable motivation for the crew to do its best and thus help maximize the film's chances for success.

Although this kind of arrangement may appear to be a serious exploitation of crew members, it can actually be mutually beneficial to both producer and crew. How else can a filmmaker with little or no money for a production get a crew? How else can inexperienced crew members get experience? Ultimately—whether the film is a success or not and to at least some extent—both sides get what they want: the filmmaker gets his film made, and the new crew members get some valuable experience that they can put on their resumes.

The film industry also has another way people work for free. They're called internships and they are often part of a formal course of study at a four-year college. Among the colleges and universities that offer such internship programs are UCLA, USC, San Francisco State University, University of Texas, and New York University. If you are interested in pursuing this path to get into the film industry, you should contact the admissions offices of colleges for more information. Appendix 3 of this book lists thirty-three organizations that offer internships.

Entering into an internship is considered by some in the business to be a noble action, because it suggests that you're so committed to the industry that you're willing to break in by working for free. The fact is, though, that many positions require training and a certain number of years of work experience. While most professional industry jobs do not require a college degree, they do require that you intern for a period of time to gain the technical, creative, and managerial skills necessary to function effectively in that field.

If you are thinking about interning in the industry, it would be advisable to give some thought to your specific area or areas of interest so that you can prepare. If, for example, you're thinking about interning as an editor, it would be a good idea to take a few editing classes at a film school. Such experience will not only make you more attractive as a candidate for an internship, but will also make you more valuable once you've begun your training.

BREAKING INTO THE INDUSTRY

No matter what your background is, if the movie business has captivated you, and you want to be involved in the filmmaking process, it is possible for you to start at the bottom, learn about the business, and work your way up to the kind of job you dream about. Most film professionals, in fact, started out as "go-fers" or production assistants. They learned the ropes, became more knowledgeable about the business, and eventually established themselves in their careers. Some of them were college graduates, and some never even graduated from high school, but they had a strong—even overwhelming—desire to be in the business. It was their persistence that kept them alive and made them successful.

There are as many stories of breaking into the industry as there are people who have done it, and no two are exactly the same. A fairly typical one, though, is the story of how James Cameron, Academy Award–winning producer and director of *Titanic*, came up through the ranks.

James Cameron's Story

Before he became involved in the film industry, James Cameron was a machinist and trucker. His first job in the industry was as a model maker on a film called *Battle Beyond the Stars*, produced by the notorious low-budget-film producer Roger Corman's New

World Pictures in 1979. As Cameron recalled that job to Paula Parisi of the Hollywood Reporter in 1995, the miniature work on the film was going well, as was the live-action set work, but director Jimmy Murakami was having trouble figuring out how to combine the two elements. Cameron convinced him that the little-used technique of front projection was the solution and that he was the man for the job. As a result, Cameron was promoted to supervisor of process projection, and four weeks later, when the art director was fired, he was asked to take that position.

Cameron's next project was as co-supervisor of visual effects on John Carpenter's 1981 film *Escape From New York*, in which he supervised model making and process photography. That project completed, Cameron moved on to *Galaxy of Terror*, also released in 1981, for which he designed the sets, miniatures, and costumes and did second-unit direction.

Cameron's first shot at the director's helm was for another independent producer. The association developed out of his tenure at New World, which had made Joe Dante's *Piranha* in 1978. Corman had sold the sequel rights to two Italian producers, who then set out to find a director for this tale of killer fish that take to the air to terrorize a beach full of bikini-clad beauties. As Cameron's luck would have it, in the course of their search they happened to visit the set of *Galaxy of Terror* while Cameron was directing a second-unit scene.

As he recounted this pivotal event in his career some years later, Cameron recalled that the scene he was directing was of a dismembered arm lying on the ground. "It's supposed to be covered with maggots," he remembered, "and they've got it covered with this tub of mealworms. You can buy them in pet stores; they're feed for fish, fairly innocuous little creatures. They're pretty law-abiding; they don't do very much . . . . They're supposed to be writhing around but they just sat there."

His solution was to run some hidden electrical wires to the worms and deliver a few inspirational jolts. Just then, the producers of the yet-to-be *Piranha II* strolled onto the set. Cameron called "Action!"—the cue for a technician hidden out of eye range to throw the juice, and "The worms start moving like crazy. I say:

'OK that's good. Cut.' He pulls the plug and the worms stop. I turn around and these two producers are just gaping. I guess they figured out that if I could get a performance out of mealworms, I should be okay with actors, so they offered me the film."

Sixteen years later, James Cameron stood on the stage of the Dorothy Chandler Pavilion and accepted the Academy Award for Best Picture of the Year—along with numerous other Oscars—for his stunning *Titanic*, which has become the highest-grossing film of all time.

Steven Spielberg's Story

Although *Titanic* holds the record for the highest gross revenues for a film, over the years Steven Spielberg has proven himself to be one of the most popular and commercially successful filmmakers in history. And while his path to success is different from Cameron's, it is just as instructive.

Spielberg studied film at California State University at Long Beach, but even while he was a student he knew he wanted to be on the Universal Studios lot, and he found an ingenious way of doing so. Wearing a suit and carrying a briefcase, he wandered onto the lot one day and made himself at home by adopting an empty office. He spent most of his time there in the editing rooms, where he was able to observe dubbing and editing. When people asked who he was, he would say, "I'm just some kid hanging around." In fact, he spent three months just "hanging around" the studio.

After making five short student films, his 24-minute movie, *Amblin'* was shown at the 1969 Atlanta Film Festival and subsequently was seen by a producer at Universal. His extraordinary talent was evident even at that very young age—he was only 21—and as a result he was given a seven-year contract with Universal, making him the youngest director ever to land a long-term deal with a major Hollywood studio. He never graduated from Cal State.

Working for Universal Television, he directed episodes of *Night Gallery; Marcus Welby, M.D.;* and *Columbo,* as well as the made-for-television feature-length films *Evil* (1971), *Savage* (1972), and *Duel* (1972). Spielberg made his feature-directing debut with *The Sugarland Express* with Goldie Hawn and subsequently directed such enormously successful films as *Close Encounters of the Third Kind* (1977), *Raiders of the Lost Ark* (1981), *E.T.—The Extraterrestrial* (1982), *The Color Purple* (1985), *Jurassic Park* (1993), and *Saving Private Ryan* (1998), among others.

Although he was nominated for several Academy Awards, he was consistently denied the prize until 1993, when his extraordinary *Schindler's List* was named Best Picture of the Year by the Motion Picture Academy.

How can you get your first job in the film industry? It may not be in the same way that either Cameron or Spielberg did it, but it can be done. In the following pages, we will look at the most popular positions within the film industry. You'll learn how to take a proactive approach to the daunting task of earning "top of the mind awareness." You'll find out how to build a network of contacts and how to keep that network working for you. You'll meet men and women who found jobs in film and hear about their experiences, their wisdom, their mistakes, and their triumphs. Whether you're in Hollywood or 1,000 miles away from the nearest studio, this book will show you how to find your way to movie productions and become a part of the magic on the screen.

chapter 2

What's Out There

In 1996, there were close to 250,000 wage and salary jobs in the motion picture production and distribution industry. The majority of those jobs were in specialty positions in motion picture production and services, including producers, directors, actors, camera operators, writers, artists and set painters, editors, and film processors, as well as specialists working in motion picture and videotape reproduction, marketing and public relations, and equipment and wardrobe rental. The freelance, contract, and part-time employment numbers are difficult to determine because neither guilds nor unions usually represent these individuals.

Many people in the film industry are self-employed, independent contractors. They market their service job-by-job to any person who requires their talent, often working on several productions in one year. For example, a set painter may work on three films a year (on average) and earn a gross annual income of $95,000. A sound recorder hired in a nonunion town may net an income of $75,000 by working on a job-to-job basis. But competition is fierce, and for most freelancers, the work takes a thick skin, rigid work standards, an ability to tolerate long hours, and a willingness to handle lowly, unglamorous tasks while trying to maintain a positive attitude. As a result, freelancers generally work only part-time schedules, which makes it extraordinarily difficult for many people to earn a living solely from their freelance work.

Another vital complication for freelancers is that many independent filmmakers maintain a list of their favorite contractors who they call frequently for projects or use for referrals when their favorites aren't available. Getting on these lists (which will be discussed later) is the most important key to getting work.

Hollywood and New York City are the primary centers for obtaining work in the production of motion pictures and films for television, although studios are also located in Florida, Texas, San Francisco, and other parts of the country. In addition, many films are shot on location throughout the United States and abroad. Production companies that shoot on location usually hire locals, unless they bring their crew with them. It is more cost-effective for the production company to hire locals, although it's common practice to bring some crew members and hire additional, local freelancers. Freelance work of this nature can be found through local film commissions or unions.

A film commission office generates revenue for its city by persuading a production to use area locations and actors for its movie and then supporting and assisting the production throughout filming. Although some cities may lack adequate film commissions, those with strong offices will also work as clearinghouses by maintaining resumes and files on local production vendors. A production company will then extract from this pool of talent and contract freelance workers for its film.

People with the same fundamental skills can create feature films, television and video productions, commercials, documentaries, music videos, and industrial (training and educational) films. Jobs fall into three phases: Preproduction, production, and postproduction. Some individuals, such as producers and directors, work in all three phases, from the beginning to the end of the production. Many producers and directors will work on a film for two years or longer.

Preproduction is the planning stage. This involves activities such as budgeting, casting, finding the right location, costume design, set design and construction, and scheduling. During the preproduction phase, the film commission is contacted to determine the shooting locations and the hiring of local vendors. Some film commissions have telephone hotline numbers, enabling vendors to call in regularly for information about ongoing local productions or production offices to which they might apply for future work.

The *production* phase begins when the cameras start to roll. The number of people involved in this phase can vary from a few for a documentary film to hundreds for a feature film. It is at this point that most freelancers want to sign on as contract workers, in hopes of being hired for the duration of the film's production phase. If they are willing to work long hours (between 12 and 16 hours a day) and do any type of work that is needed, even menial tasks, the likelihood is that they will be on the production until it leaves town. They also stand a better chance of being hired again for another film, if the production company returns to that city.

Postproduction activities take place in the editing rooms and recording studios, where the film is shaped into its final form. The postproduction stage can make or break a film. Some filmmakers call this process their last rewrite of the movie. There are times when a film in "post" has to go back to the production phase to clarify or enhance a story line that may not be working. As this can be very costly for the producer, he or she will try to avoid it by ensuring that the production starts out with a complete and carefully crafted script (although, as you will see, even that is subject to change).

Even before a film moves into the preproduction phase, it begins with an idea that scriptwriters turn into a script. The idea might be an original one or an existing literary work that is adapted into a screenplay. Scriptwriters work closely with producers and directors. Sometimes they prepare a shooting script that has instructions for camera angles and shots, as well as lighting. They frequently make changes to the script to reflect the directors' and producers' ideas and desires. In fact, most scripts are rewritten several times before production begins. Many scriptwriters make a living doing rewrites, for which they usually don't receive screen credit but do get a handsome paycheck.

Thus, a scriptwriter is required not only to have a good imagination and be able to come up with story ideas but also to be willing and able to write and rewrite many script versions under pressure. Scriptwriting is an excellent way to learn about the filmmaking or television production process and to explore other jobs in the film industry. Many directors and producers started out as scriptwriters.

Feature film writers work on a freelance basis and usually have many years of experience under their belts. Most likely they started their careers by writing "spec" scripts—that is, a story in script format that is dear to their hearts or that they think can be a commercial success. An agent or attorney then submits the script to a large number of production companies, where readers evaluate its quality and write a summary of the story. Producers often make their decision about whether or not to buy a script based on the reader's report.

Interestingly, most writers who sell a spec script are not hired to write the final version; instead, it is put into the hands of an experienced feature film writer. So how do you progress from spec scripts to shooting scripts? For many successful scriptwriters, the key has been to have mentors who taught them the art of screenwriting by going over the spec script with a keen and critical eye and helping to turn it into a real, usable script. These mentors can also serve as references when an ambitious writer wants to move to the next echelon of scriptwriting.

To subsidize their incomes, scriptwriters often start as copywriters in advertising agencies or writers for educational film companies, government audiovisual departments, or in-house corporate film divisions. These jobs not only serve as a good training ground for beginners but also have greater job security than freelancing. One aspiring writer subsidizes her income with market research and market report writing. Another works for the state legislature analyzing future mandates and writing summaries for the law-making body.

Preproduction Occupations

Producers are those individuals who look for properties or ideas that they believe can be turned into lucrative film projects or television shows. A property, for example, might be the rights to dramatize a headline news story or retell a historical event (e.g., *Apollo 13* or *Titanic*). Ideas, on the other hand, can come from any source and are much easier to obtain, unless they've already been written in treatment form and registered as copyrighted material. Producers may see numerous films, read a great number of scripts, periodicals, and trade magazines, and maintain a network of contacts with literary editors and agents, Hollywood brokers, and publishers. They stay in the know on current events and trends because they don't want to miss the opportunity for a mega-hit movie for a summer, a year, or a decade.

Producers put together the financing for a production and are responsible for all financial aspects of a film. These responsibilities include working closely with the director on the selection of a script, casting the principal roles, and identifying locations for filming—all decisions that greatly affect the cost of making a movie. Once financing is obtained for a picture, the producer works out a detailed budget and sees to it that the production costs stay within the budget. In a large production, the producer also works closely with the production managers who are in charge of crews, travel, casting, and equipment.

An independent producer may hire a large number of neophyte freelance workers on a project that requires a lot of person-hours. The producer may need only seven new people but will hire ten because he knows that some will not be able to make the grade. Usually, by the end of the first day, he will let two or three workers go and end up with the dedicated, hard-working people he really needs.

Art directors design the physical environment of the film set in order to create the mood the script calls for. They supervise many different people, such as illustrators, scenic designers, model makers, carpenters, painters, electricians, laborers, set decorators, costume designers, animal makers, and makeup and hairstyling artists. These positions can provide an entry to the motion picture industry in major cities or at a film location shooting. Many start in these jobs in live theater productions and then move back and forth between the stage, film, and television. For these people, happiness is working in the entertainment field and making a living at what they like to do best.

Location scouts or *location managers* work with the art director and director to find the ideal location for a particular shot in a scene. Location scouts are hired early in the preproduction phase of the movie. Nathan, who is a location scout in the Eldorado Hills of northern California, feels location scouting is a true art form.

"You are trying to interpret the script while finding the right location that can make all the difference in the movie."

While it's true that the art director and director get all the credit, it all starts with the ingenuity of the location scout. The location scout will find the location for the director and then get her/his approval. Usually, the same person will switch hats and become the location manager. The location manager handles all the logistics of using the location, such as permits and approval from local governments. Whenever problems arise on location, it's the location manager's responsibility to handle them. Nathan says the job offers a lot of independence—you're pretty much your own boss.

The *casting director* is another preproduction job that requires a strong understanding of the script and a keen eye for talent. Directors set guidelines for the "types" they are looking for and the casting director selects actors and brings them to audition for the director, who makes the final selection. It's important that he knows the actors' abilities and can communicate them to the director. The director, in turn, must provide feedback to the casting director, so the casting director knows whether he/she is on the right track.

Production Occupations

Directors are the individuals who "translate" the script from the written page into a film. To do this, a typical director may supervise hundreds of people at a time, from scriptwriters to costume and set designers. Directors are in charge of all technical and artistic aspects of the film. They conduct auditions, supervise rehearsals, and approve location, scenery, costumes, choreography, and music. In short, they direct the entire cast and crew during shooting. They frequently have several assistant directors helping them with such details as handling extras, transporting equipment, and arranging for food and accommodations.

In general, the job of director is not an entry-level position. Usually, individuals who want to become directors start in another phase of filmmaking and use their experience and varied job opportunities to eventually advance to directing. Music videos can also provide experience for budding directors.

Successful directors are involved in all three phases of production, from beginning to end. Some directors assume multiple roles, such as director-producer, writer-producer-director, or even actor-writer-producer-director. Whatever other roles they take on, as directors they must know how to hire the right people, how to fire the wrong people, and how to handle people so that they work as an effective team. They must often combine the skills of an artist, administrator, salesperson, diplomat, and best friend.

In the autumn of 1973, Elia Kazan, director of such classic films as *Gentleman's Agreement*, *A Streetcar Named Desire*, and *On the Waterfront*, was honored by a two-week retrospective of his films at Wesleyan University in Middletown, Connecticut. At the conclusion of the program, Mr. Kazan gave a talk to the students, during which he spoke about the role of a director.

"What kind of person must a film director train himself to be? What qualities does he need?" he asked. "Here are a few: A construction gang foreman, who knows his physical problems and their solutions and is ready, therefore, to insist on these solutions . . . A hypnotist, who works with the unconscious to achieve his ends. A poet, a poet of the camera, able both to capture the decisive moment of Cartier Bresson or to wait all day like Paul Strand for a single shot, which he makes with a bulky camera fixed on a tripod. An outfielder, for his legs. The director stands much of the day, dares not get tired, so he has strong legs. Think back and remember how the old time directors dramatized themselves. By puttees, right?

"He also needs the cunning of a trader in a Baghdad bazaar. The firmness of an animal trainer. Obvious. Tigers! A great host. At a sign from him, fine food and heartwarming drink appear. The kindness of an old-fashioned mother who forgives all. The authority and sternness of her husband, the father, who forgives nothing, expects obedience without question, brooks no nonsense. These alternatively. The elusiveness of a jewel thief—no explanation, take my word for this one. The blarney of a PR man, especially useful when the director is out in a strange and hostile location, as I have many times been. A very thick skin. A very sensitive soul. Simultaneously. The patience, the persistence, the fortitude of a saint, the appreciation of pain, a taste for self-sacrifice, everything for the cause. Cheeriness, jokes, playfulness, alternating with sternness, unwavering firmness. Pure doggedness. An unwavering refusal to take less than he thinks right out of a scene, a performer, a co-worker, a member of his staff, himself."

Actors, of course, perform in front of the cameras rather than behind the scenes, but it's important to know about the jobs that *actors* do—especially as some very famous ones have become writers, producers, and directors (and combinations thereof). It is, in fact, becoming quite commonplace for actors to take on multiple roles in a film, both behind and in front of the camera. Prime examples of these "Renaissance people" include stars such as Paul Newman, Robert Redford, Woody Allen, Angelica Huston, Tim Robbins, Goldie Hawn, Diane Keaton, and Mel Gibson.

Actors entertain and communicate with the audience through their interpretation of dramatic or comedic roles. Only a small number achieve a tremendous amount of recognition in motion pictures. Some start as "extras" (the people in the background of a film) with no lines to deliver, while others are cast in supporting roles or as walk-ons. A "feature extra" may be used for the same film over and over again, with no lines but lots of camera time. Stunt people take on the more dangerous work, performing such stunts as driving cars in chase scenes, falling from buildings and other high places, or "fighting" in place of the principal actors.

Most acting jobs are found through agents. Beginners and lesser-known actors who are nonunion will usually register themselves, for a slight fee, with several casting directors. They are then invited to auditions, which may lead to acting assignments.

Although a few actors and actresses find parts in feature films straight out of drama school, most spend many years supporting themselves by working at jobs inside or outside the industry. To learn the ropes, some actors and actresses have obtained jobs at talent agencies or casting companies. Here they learn the process of setting up auditions and casting for commercials, film, and television.

Cinematographers (or directors of photography), *camera operators,* and *gaffers* work together as a team to interpret the scenes in the script and put them on film. The cinematographer supervises lighting and the set-up of camera shots. Lighting and filters help the cinematographer compose shots that will reflect the mood the director wishes to create. The camera operator handles all camera movements, as well as the focusing and actual shooting. Assistant camera operators check the equipment, load the camera, operate the slate and clapsticks, and take care of the equipment. The gaffer is the chief electrician and is responsible for the lighting of the scenes.

Sound engineers, recordists, and boom operators record dialogue, sounds, music, and special effects during the filming. Sound engineers are the "ears" of the film. They supervise all the sound generated during filming. They also select all the microphones and gauge the level of sound from mixers and synthesizers to ensure the best sound quality. Recordists help set up the equipment and are in charge of the individual tape recorders. Boom operators handle long booms with microphones that are moved from one area of the set to another. Because more and more filming is done on location, and the equipment has become more compact, lighter, and simpler to operate, one person often performs many of the above functions. However, sound recordists and boom operators sometimes team up and get jobs together, occasionally even forming their own companies.

Special effects technicians are responsible for the movie "magic." Through their imagination, versatility, and skill, they can create anything required by the scripts, from monsters and talking animals to flaming office buildings and earthquakes. Many begin as stage technicians or scenic designers doing menial jobs. A special effects technician not only needs a good imagination but also must be part carpenter, plumber, electrician, and electronics expert. These workers have to be familiar with many ways of achieving a desired special effect, because each movie usually requires different skills or talents.

Computer skills have become very important in the field of special effects. Some areas of film production, including animation and visual effects, now rely heavily on computer technology, with a corresponding decrease in the need for production specialists. For example, some specialists create "synthespians"—realistic digital humans—that appear mainly in science fiction productions. These lifelike digital images are often used when a particular scene is too dangerous for an actor or even a stunt person. In *Titanic*, for example, James Cameron used "synthespians" for the bodies that are hurled into the water just before the ship sinks.

Many individuals get started in these various occupations by just helping out on sets and in studios: running errands, moving things, helping with props, or doing whatever else is needed. In essence, they start out as apprentices and gradually move up through the ranks—which is hard work in itself and not very lucrative. An apprentice generally begins as a "flat"—that is, a neophyte who works for a flat fee of $50 for the whole day, or until he or she drops from exhaustion. Those who stick with it can find success and rewards, because they're working at a job they love to do in an industry that provides both variety and excitement.

Postproduction Occupations

Film editors are the people who really put a movie together, so theirs is one of the most important tasks in filmmaking and television production. After the film is shot and processed, editors study the footage, select the best shots, and assemble them in the most effective way. Their goal is to create dramatic continuity, the right pace, and the desired mood.

To accomplish their objectives, editors first organize the footage and then structure the sequence of the film by splicing and re-splicing the best shots. They not only must have a good eye but also must understand the subject of the film and what the director has in mind. In fact, they often work closely with the director in this process.

Assistant editors or dubbing editors then select the sound track and special sound effects to produce the final combination of sight and sound as it appears on the screen. Editing room assistants help with the splicing, patching, rewinding, coding, and storing of the film. They work long hours with a lot of overtime, often because the job is on a tight deadline for a special screening and the film must be ready by a certain date. Some television networks have film librarians who are responsible for organizing, cataloging, filing, and selecting footage for the film editors.

Many editors enter the business by working as go-fers or production assistants, doing odd jobs as needed. In fact, editors are always in need of help. Some successful editors started out by volunteering their help on a film, which resulted in their being hired onto the production. As you'll recall from the first chapter, Steven Spielberg started his career at Universal Studios by helping out in the film editing department. But while there is no one sure way of entering the occupation of editor, experience as a film librarian, sound editor, or assistant editor—plus talent and perseverance—usually helps.

Sound effects editors or *audio recording engineers* do some of the final jobs in post-production. These workers add prerecorded and live sound effects and background music by manipulating various elements of music, dialogue, and background sound to fit the picture, often using such techniques as automated dialogue replacement (ADR) and working with a Foley mixer. Their work has become increasingly computer-driven as electronic equipment has replaced conventional tape recording devices. The best way to get into sound work in film is through experience at radio stations, with music groups, in music videos, or by adding audio to Internet sites.

Once a film is finished, it's time to implement a *marketing* strategy for it. The people who work in this area estimate the demand for the film and the audience to whom it will appeal, then develop an advertising and promotion plan and decide where and when to release the film. *Advertising workers* or *unit publicists* write press releases and short biographies of actors, actresses, and directors for newspapers and magazines. They may also set up interviews or television appearances for the stars or director to promote a film. *Sales workers* sell the finished product. Many production companies have their own staff to distribute, lease, and sell their films and made-for-television programs to theater owners and television networks. The best way to enter sales work in films is to start by selling advertising time for television or radio stations and nurturing the contacts you make that way.

Finally, large film and television studios are headed by a *chief executive officer* (CEO) who is responsible to a board of directors and stockholders. Financial managers, business managers, accountants, and lawyers report to the CEO. However, small film companies, and those in business and educational film production, cannot afford to have so many different people, each handling only one aspect of the business. Thus, they are usually headed by an owner-producer who originates, develops, produces, and distributes films with just a basic staff of freelance workers.

These small companies offer good training opportunities to beginners because they provide exposure to many phases of film and television production. Most of the freelancers are hired because of recommendations from other freelance workers, i.e., "I know this guy who is looking for some work. He did an excellent job on an independent film with Sayles that I worked on last week. You should give him a call. Here's his number."

So how do you make it as a freelancer or contractor in the film business? The key is in getting that first job. Once you're hired, you can work hard and show what you're capable of doing. After that, the chances are good that you'll be called back for more work—and then you'll *really* love the business!

chapter 3

The Bottom Up

Finding a job in the film industry is rather like trying to find a sunken vessel lost at sea: it is not only difficult, it is an art. This is because the movie-making business is a hidden market. Employers and employees rely on reputation, word-of-mouth, and networking as their primary tools of communication. By the time a project comes to town or starts production in a major city, positions are usually already filled.

The nature of producing a movie (and obtaining the related jobs) is that it is short-term and project-oriented. As a rule, film producers and directors are independent contractors. Few companies other than major networks can afford to maintain a director or crew on permanent payroll. People who do have permanent jobs don't give them up. As one director put it, "Even when they die, they try to pass their job on to someone in their family."

It's not only who you know and what you know, but what you have done and what you have done lately. In other words, you are always positioning yourself for the next job while maintaining your current job. If you are smart and maintain a positive attitude, you don't burn your bridges behind you, making it impossible to return. Instead, you use your current experience to build toward the next one. This is why ignorance of the nature of the business and how hiring really works can make your efforts fall flat and be unprofitable. We'll start by taking a look at what are considered some of the most popular but ineffective strategies people use in attempting to secure employment in the film industry, as well as some of the most creative and effective strategies.

First, what strategies don't necessarily work? Unsolicited resumes (also known as junk mail to some producers and directors) have their place, but most newcomers can't afford to send out enough resumes to obtain the ideal opportunity for a quality interview. The fact is, if a job seeker is lucky, the resume will be placed on file in a dark, deep cabinet in the personnel department.

Jobs advertised in the classifieds are generally filled by the time the ad appears in the papers. Many personnel departments advertise jobs as a matter of course to satisfy their equal opportunity requirements. This makes it possible for them to prove beyond a shadow of a doubt that the job was open before anyone was hired by simply showing the resumes received before the date of hire.

The myth that "If I sleep with the producer, director, or casting director, I get the job" is just that—a myth. How could directors or casting directors possibly hang their careers on a one-night stand? Too much depends on the quality of work expected from their cast and crew to permit a roll in the hay to jeopardize their professional futures. Of course, there are exceptions to this, and some ambitious people do use the "casting couch" to get ahead. But these people are few and far between, and do not reflect the reality of getting a job in the film industry.

ACT LIKE A PRO BEFORE YOU'RE A PRO

Before you are hired, you may be tempted to make statements such as: "I don't pick up garbage," "I don't get coffee," "I don't run errands," "I don't get dry cleaning," "I've already paid my dues," "I have to leave by six," "I can't work overtime because I have an appointment to get my nails done," "I'm a single mother," or "I have a life." If you're going to do this, then don't even bother going to the interview—the film industry is simply not for you. What you need is a nine-to-five job, whereas in film and television work, people are always adjusting their schedules. They never know when they will be home, and typically work a 10- to 12-hour day. When they are on a project, they don't see their families until the project is done. Most important, they love every minute of it!

Acting like a student or intern—even when you are a student or intern—will destroy your hopes for success faster than not showing up for work. The moment you are hired on to a set, you are a professional. The idea that "I am not going to act like a professional because I am not being paid enough to be a professional (or I am not being paid at all)" is the iceberg that will sink your chances for a career in film.

Professionals are people who can produce high-quality work, regardless of other considerations. It never enters their heads that they are just there for the ride, or that it's enough just to be on the set and experience the so-called glamour of the film world. A professional knows the rules of the game as a matter of course and will seek to achieve the highest quality in his or her work. That means consistently striving to be the best at whatever you do and convincing your employer that it is not only worth it to keep you on this job but also to hire you for the next one.

BUILDING CREDITS

But how do you get the "first job" that gets your foot inside the door? We have already discussed several ways: internships, volunteering, and demonstrating the ability to do whatever is needed and then doing it well.

Most important to the process, however, is that you have to be willing—in the beginning, at least—to work on the cheap or even for free. The idea is to accumulate a list of "credits"—that is, all your past work experience. You can only do this by being willing to take on whatever work is being offered at whatever pay is being offered, even if that's zero. Of course, even if you offer your services for free, you may still find it hard to attract any takers, as even an unpaid crew member needs to be covered by insurance, shown the ropes, fed, etc.

Your best opportunity to build up your credits list is to work on smaller independent shoots. Track these shoots down and volunteer! Once your resume begins to show the depth of your experience, you can start to aim for bigger crews on larger shoots.

It is best to start making contacts in your local area. You can contact your local film commission and see if they have a hotline number or a Web site. Most big city film commissions do. Check with your film commission once a week to find out if a production company is coming to town. Sometimes the production companies will leave a contact number with the film commission. You can contact local casting directors and see if they know of any production companies coming to town. As you call these contacts, make sure you find out about other production contacts. Here are some general numbers and Web sites to contact for information on film work in the area. (Appendix 1 of this book provides a comprehensive listing of key film employers.)

- **California Film Commission**—800-858-4749
  http://commerce.ca.gov/business/select/film

- **San Francisco Film Commission Hotline**—415-554-4004
  http://commerce.ca.gov/regional/bayarea

- **Los Angeles Film Commission**—626-683-2619
  http://commerce.ca.gov/regional/losangeles

- **New York Film Commission**—212-803-2330
  http://www.empire.state.ny.us/

- **New York City Film Commission**—212-489-6710
  http://www.ci.nyc.ny.us/

- **Orlando Film Commission**—407-422-7159
  http://www.film-orlando.org/foffc/fa_foffc.htm

- **Texas Film Commission**—512-463-9200
  http://www.governor.state.tx.us/film/

There are also Web sites that are resources for getting work in film production. Each one is different and independently produced. Some require that you subscribe to their newsletter or become a member.

- **Showbiz Jobs**
  http://www.showbizjobs.com
  —a membership is required

- *Production Weekly*
  http://www.productionweekly.com

—offers up-to-date information on film, commercial, and television productions and is published every Thursday

- **ESP NET, INC**
  espnet@earthlink.net
  —contact them by e-mail or ground mail:
    Box 663
    Culver City, CA 90232-0663
  —they send out a newsletter every month

- **Listing of Major Production Companies**
  http://theinkwell.com/guide/prodcos.html
  —this is just what it says

- **Maslow Media Group Job Hotline**
  301-570-9100 for CREW & TALENT
  http://www.maslowmedia.com

There are also a number of hotlines that can provide leads for jobs.

- **E! Entertainment Television Internship Hotline**
  Los Angeles: 213-954-2710

- **E! Entertainment Television Jobline**
  Los Angeles: 213-954-2666

- **Paramount Studios Jobline**
  Los Angeles: 213-956-5216

- **Lorimar Studios**
  Los Angeles: 818-954-5400

- **Disney Studios**
  Burbank, CA: 818-558-2222

- **Amblin Entertainment (Dreamworks)**
  Los Angeles: 818-777-4600

- **New Line Cinema**
  Los Angeles: 310-967-6553

- **Polygram**
  Los Angeles: 213-856-2729

- **Sony**
  Los Angeles: 310-280-4436

- **Spelling Entertainment**
  Los Angeles: 213-634-3700

- **FOX**
  Los Angeles: 310-369-2804

- **Universal Studios**
  Los Angeles: 818-777-5627

- **Warner Brothers Studios**
  Los Angeles: 818-954-5400

- **Turner**
  Los Angeles: 310-788-4255

Contrary to popular belief, many people in the film and video industry like to give new people a break, but you'll need to impress them with your keenness, enthusiasm, and hard work. Always remember that although you're working for free, you're not doing the production a favor—they're doing you one.

Eventually, if you work hard enough and do a good enough job, you'll find yourself being offered regular paid work when it's available. The time may even come when an outsider desperate to work on a crew approaches you.

Another key to getting work is knowing how to cultivate the people you meet. In the film industry, it is just as important to gain expertise in public relations as it is to gain expertise in the technology of the business. Technology is easy. People are tough. They want to make money, but they also want to have a good time while they're doing it.

Hollywood is famous for its get-to-know-you lunches. People in Hollywood want to know you before they work with you. No other field has people with bigger egos or bigger dreams, working on larger budgets (real and imagined), against more impossible deadlines, with bigger stakes, higher rates of return (real and imagined), and greater likelihood of disaster. Every production is a custom job that can be placed in jeopardy with one bad attitude, one miscommunication, or one slip of the tongue. Because of the large number of people involved in a production, there are too many variables that can slow it down or completely stop it in its tracks. Your goal on your first job, then, is twofold: Do your job well and fit in!

Many of the producers, directors, actors, and crew that "click" together will stay together, production after production. Once they find a "winning team," they are not about to change it. Clint Eastwood has used the same editor for 20 years. Sidney Pollack has made at least four films with Robert Redford. Tom Hanks has worked with Steven Spielberg twice. Woody Allen uses the same production assistants over and over, as well as the same cameraman and editor.

One thing to bear in mind as you enter into film work is that the entertainment world is filled to the brim with temperamental people. We all have good days and bad days, of course, so ask yourself, "How will my attitude affect my ability to work long days and to perform as a team player?" In other words, do you have what it takes to deal with exhausting schedules and a wide variety of egos and temperaments? If you feel at all uneasy as you consider that question, then you should closely examine your decision to go into this field. But if you really love the business in spite of it all and can't think of anything else you would rather do for the rest of your life, then, by all means, stick with it and have a fantastic time doing it!

SET ETIQUETTE

Once you start getting work, you want to continue to be offered jobs. This means you have to develop a reputation, not just for hard work but also for your attitude and cooperation during the production. The key here is to gain a good understanding of set etiquette. Once you know the ins and outs of proper behavior on the set, you will probably never have to worry again about getting fired or not being called back for the next day's work.

Many people outside the film industry assume that a film set is an exciting, dynamic place, where artists of equal standing share in and contribute to the making of the film. The public often imagines a director calmly chatting with the actors and department heads about the script, the costumes, the set design, or the lighting and mulling over issues of form and color, drama and performance. They assume that the shoot is a creative and democratic process. Well, in a way it is—but not all sets are alike. For the most part, a film production is a high-pressure, high-tension experience, filled with many variables and more grunt work than creativity. In fact, most of the really creative work takes place during preproduction or postproduction. The production itself is the process of getting the job done after weeks of planning. The director and crew are struggling against time and budget to put the story on the screen according to a plan. The only creative process going on involves decisions to solve the innumerable problems that come up during a shoot.

This is why it can be said that filmmaking is about dictatorship. To keep a production under control, it has to have its chain of command, complete with its minions (crew), mini-emperors (department heads), and supreme dictator (the director). Ideally, the shoot is a good and benign dictatorship. The crew admires and respects their leaders, and the leaders all get along with each other. On occasion, however, it may become more of a fascist dictatorship, with petty power battles and backstabbing politics. Regardless of the style, one thing remains constant: the shoot is a dictatorship, and if you want to survive on set, you need to know some basic set etiquette.

Six Rules for Building a Good Reputation Early in Your Career

Rule Number 1

Always arrive early; never arrive late. If the crew call is for 6 A.M., strive to get there at 5:30 or 5:45 A.M.. Not only will you impress the director or producer, but you will also get a fresh breakfast. You can chat with other crew members (especially those you normally wouldn't talk to), and you can be among the first to know what's in store for the day. You might even be called upon to do something that will attract attention to your dedication and enthusiasm for the job. Most important, if you aim to get there early and something delays you, then you'll still be on time—and many directors place great value on promptness.

Rule Number 2

Don't wander away from the set, even if you are idle at the moment. It's important that you always be close at hand to do your job the instant you are told to do something. If you must leave the set—to go to the bathroom, for instance, or to get a drink of water—do it quickly and hurry back. Even low-budget films consume hundreds of dollars every minute of every day during the shoot. If you aren't there when you're needed and another crew member has to search for you, it eats up time, which costs the production hundreds if not thousands of dollars. This is why you always see people standing around on a film set. It may seem at first to be a waste of money, but in reality they are being paid to be available on a moment's call.

Rule Number 3

Always look busy when you are on the set. This applies to most jobs in the real world, but especially to filmmaking. No matter how many hours you have been slaving away, hauling lighting gear, or moving props, the moment you sit down for a break is the moment the director or producer walks past and thinks, "Am I paying that bum to just sit there all day?"

Rule Number 4

Don't talk to other departments unless told to do so. This probably seems illogical to you, but it's a fact: you never deal directly with another crew member from a different department, because it's not your job to do so. For example, if you are an assistant sound recordist, it may seem reasonable for you to ask one of the lighting crew about moving a noisy light. But if you do this, you may be contradicting an order given by your boss, which results in miscommunications and delays, which in turn costs the production money. You can't take independent action—you must go through the proper command channels. If you have a problem involving another department, speak to your senior about it. Your senior will then speak to his or her senior, who will speak to his or her department head, and so on until the problem is resolved. Yes, it's a frustrating way to go, but it's necessary in a dictatorship. With the large number of people involved in a film production, there has to be a clear understanding of who does what and who reports to whom and a rigid adherence to the command structure. It is the only way to prevent chaos and to keep people focused on what they're supposed to be doing. Of course, safety is the exception to the rule. If you see a crew member in danger, then etiquette does not apply. Help him or her immediately.

Rule Number 5

Don't be a clock-watcher. Whether you are being paid by the hour or doing the job for love, time is not supposed to matter to you. When a shoot runs over time, everybody is expected to stay; neither the director nor the department heads want to hear any moaning about it. Not only is it unpleasant to order around unwilling crew members, but they may also end up with a negative opinion of you if your attitude is betrayed by spoken word or body language. If a department head or director thinks that you aren't enthusiastic or willing, then you won't be asked to work for them the next time. Thus, when you're asked to keep working an extra 2 to 3 hours—and you will be!—be prepared to drop whatever you may have planned and lie, if need be. Just put on a smile and say, "Sure, no problem. What's the next shot?"

Rule Number 6

Stay calm on the set, no matter what happens. Sometimes actors, crew members, department heads, and even directors let the pressure of the shoot get to them and begin behaving irrationally, even unfairly. If you can't handle stress, or can't handle it when others take their stress out on you, then you've got no place on a film set. If someone angrily chews your head off about something you have or have not done, don't bite back—rise above it. Stay calm and civilized (even if you are in the right), and ask them what they want you to do. If it's your boss or senior doing the yelling, then do what he or she asks, and do it quickly, without getting angry or upset (however difficult that may be). If the angry person is not part of your chain of command, then check with your boss or senior before you do anything. If you can weather the storm, it will pass. Chances are you'll find that it had nothing at all to do with you personally. By staying calm in these confrontational situations, you not only prevent yourself from stressing out but you make yourself look good and the other person look a bit foolish. (And chances are pretty good that that person will forget all about it, and give you a big hug at the wrap party!)

BOB'S STORY

Five years ago, Bob worked for a bookstore chain in Sacramento, California. He was earning $18,000 a year. Today, he earns $75,000 a year, after taxes.

How did he do it? Bob began working as a production assistant for industrial films, then worked for free on a local independent film. He took whatever work he could find, no matter what it entailed (for example, craft services, which involved maintaining a table of snacks on the set between meal periods). In time, with the contacts he made in the business, he started getting better jobs. Finally he decided on one particular direction: he wanted to be a sound recordist. Still, he couldn't always get work in that field, so he continued to do other jobs in order to keep his networking and experience current and to add to his credits.

Bob has seen a lot of people come and go in the film world. It has a high turnover rate. People let the supposed glamour of the business go to their heads. He spoke of a friend, "Sam," whom he brought into the business through a major commercial. Sam liked the work and decided his goal was to become an assistant director (AD). He refused, though, to take other jobs like craft services because, as he said, "I am an AD. I don't pick up trash. It doesn't pay very much." His ego led him to believe he was too good for certain jobs; his self-importance button was getting the best of him. "I am in the film business," he would boast, as if this made him more special than others. After two years of this attitude, he stopped getting calls for AD work.

Bob, on the other hand, loves his work. Competition is fierce. He is on call 24 hours a day, and that's fine by him. He joined a union, which has been good for him because both the pay and the working conditions are much better. Working as a union member has its perks, too. Bob gets paid for using his car, as well as for when meal breaks are late, when he works overtime, and when there's a short turn-around call. A crew normally has a 12-hour turn-around time for the next day's shoot. If, however, you're called back sooner, that's considered a short turn-around, and the production has to pay the crew extra wages.

Bob has his resume filed at the local film commission, but the bulk of his work is generated through referrals. He is sometimes amazed at who recommends him for jobs, especially when they're people who work in other niches of the business. If a production company decides to shoot in the area where Bob lives, Bob either gets a call from the company or from the location scout. He has three location scouts keeping him abreast of production work in his area. Bob doesn't have too many job interviews. He is usually hired on the recommendations of his contacts. If the director sees he has made the grade, then he's called back. He tends to veer away from the movie market. He does more commercials because commercials are shorter and the money is better. When he works on a film, he is committed to a minimum of 18 days, while commercials take no longer than four days, so he can get more work over the course of a year.

He does have those occasional job interviews. When *The Second Civil War,* an HBO cable movie (executive producer Barry Levinson, director Joe Dante) came to town, he interviewed for the craft services position, and it went great because Bob had his resume to back him up, showing he had done craft services before. Bob feels the most important thing for survival in the business is the ability and willingness to be versatile. You have to be able to do a lot of different things well—and conduct yourself as a professional as you do all of them.

Bob believes in staying in one market and working that market thoroughly. You really have to know your market, and your market has to know you. It helps to find your niche and stay in that area, or you risk losing your spot in that niche by trying something else.

One of Bob's most memorable jobs was working as a driver for director John Frankenheimer *(The Manchurian Candidate; Wallace).* "He always wanted me to hit the gas. He's into race car driving and likes to go fast. He is really a nice man."

Yes, there are perks, but Bob would be the first to say that his career is characterized first and foremost by hard work.

HELEN'S STORY

Helen's background is in theater and performance art, where she's worked as a writer, director, and performer. For eight years, she lived and struggled as an artist in New York City before she decided to go back to California.

Shortly after her return to the West Coast, Helen ran into an old acquaintance from the theater world, who hired her to work at his digital imaging production company. Her tasks involved sweeping floors, making coffee, painting walls, and cleaning toilets, among other "grunt" tasks. She kept her attitude up and her flexibility high.

It was during this challenging and exciting phase of her life that Helen discovered the joys of animation production. Working on a live-action commercial provides, at most, a week or two of employment. An animated commercial provides eight to twelve weeks of production work. Helen thought, "I really do love cartoons." So off she went to learn all the ins and outs of paper and paint.

Thanks to her contacts at the imaging company, Helen was able to present her credentials for a position as an animation production manager, and she got the job! She's been doing it now for six years, expanding her knowledge to embrace traditional animation and computer animation until she became responsible for the overall production of commercials, music videos, and television. This includes handling the budget and schedule while attending to the diverse needs of anxious producers, directors, and exhausted crew.

Helen is happy with her digital media work because she has a steady job that pays well and she's doing what she loves the most—art. Her "breakthrough technique" for success? Be willing to do the dirty work in the beginning, and be willing to build up more than one skill thereafter.

chapter 4

Put It in Writing

Getting strangers to recognize that you're serious about having a career in the film industry is what breaking into film is all about. In every job search activity—whether it's written communications, telephone conversations, or interviews—your goal is to create a positive impression that will motivate decision makers to invest more time in you and help you further your career. You have to think of yourself as a business and be willing and able to market, promote, and sell yourself. Whom to contact, how to contact them, and what to say on the telephone and in interviews will be covered in the next chapter, but for now we're going to concentrate on written communications.

People who make hiring decisions at production companies like to meet you on paper whether they have met you in person or not, and the two primary ways of introducing yourself to them are through resumes and letters. Both say a great deal about you. They reveal your communications skills as well as something of your personality. They also demonstrate, when appropriate, whether you've taken the time to research the position you're interested in. The effectiveness of your written communications can, in fact, determine your future career in the film industry.

RESUMES

Always remember that there are lots of people out there who have the same skills and the same desire to land a job in the film industry that you do. Your immediate goal is to get an interview, and your resume is one of the tools you use to do that. You'll be able to put together an effective resume if you follow these simple rules.

Rule Number 1

Make it look professional. The film industry is a professional environment, and a clean, crisp laser-printed copy is one of the most important factors in getting your resume read. The paper should be one color—white is always safe, but buff or off-white gives better results—and between 20 and 24 pounds in weight. Linen paper is the best quality. You should also proofread it, several times, and have a friend proofread it as well. Typographical errors can turn people off, and that's the last thing you want your resume to do.

Rule Number 2

Make it readable. It's important that the information on your resume be presented as clearly and succinctly as possible. Ideally, it should not be more than one page in length. If after writing it you have any doubts about its clarity—or even if you don't—it would be a good idea to have a friend look it over. Most resumes are done in one of two type sizes—10 or 12 point. It's advisable to do it in 12-point type, if everything will still fit on one page, because it's larger and easier to read. You may also want to use a larger type size for your name and address.

Rule Number 3

Tell the truth. There is a temptation, especially when you're just starting out, to stretch the truth a little in order to make yourself look more appealing to whomever will be reading your resume. As far as that's concerned, I have one word of advice: Don't! Many film production professionals stress the importance of being honest. If you worked on a film, make sure it's there on your resume. But if you didn't, don't even think about putting it down. It's easy for people to check on you, and you're bound to get caught. Remember that people like to work with people they can trust.

Here is a resume of someone who is just starting out in the business.

Jane Doe

5555 Wilshire Boulevard
Los Angeles, California 55555
E-mail: jane@internet.com
Phone: 213-555-3333
Pager: 555-555-2222

OBJECTIVE

Internship or entry-level position in film production

EDUCATION

University of California, Berkeley
B.A., Filmmaking, June 1999

WORK EXPERIENCE

Girl Friday at KWWW-TV, Dodge City, Nevada
Part-time, 6/96–9/98. Ran errands and helped with
pre-production.
Soccer Coach for all-girls team, Dodge City, Nevada
Part-time, 6/95–9/97. Coached team of 10- to 12-year-olds
to state championship.

SKILLS

Knowledge of film and broadcast equipment
Conversational Spanish
Computer, word processing, and typing

ACTIVITIES

Varsity Soccer Team
Spanish Club
Film Studies

INTERESTS

Filmmaking, soccer, bicycling, and music

You will of course have to update your resume as the situation requires. If, for example, you change your address, e-mail address, or telephone number, don't forget to change it on your resume. Equally important, as you gain experience in the business, you'll have to add that information to the resume—every bit of additional experience makes you that much more marketable, and you want to make sure that whoever sees your resume will know about it. Finally, as long as you follow the three rules above, you'll not only have a resume you can be proud of but also one that will impress its reader with your professionalism.

LETTERS

After the resume, letters are the second major means of presenting yourself in writing to potential employers and, like resumes, can make an enduring impression on their readers. Effective letters involve more than demonstrating excellent writing style on flowery paper. For the most part, your letters need to be intelligently produced and directed to the specific concerns of your potential employer. Most important, they must be followed-up with telephone calls. Bypass any one of these letter-writing stages and you'll have wasted a lot of precious time and money, which you can't afford to do. Just to give you an idea of why writing effective letters is important, here's a taste of how things happen in the real world.

When a production company is given final approval to start producing its film, the first thing it does is open a production office. Every production office has a post office box, phone number, and fax machine. Word gets around that Mr. Gotbucks is hiring gaffers, electricians, production assistants, and so forth. The resumes start flowing in like postcard entries for the *Regis and Kathy Lee Live* Hawaiian Luau Contest. The post office box is jammed each morning when the assistant producer stops by to pick up the mail on the way to the office. And at the office itself, the "in" tray of the fax machine has overflowed, sending letters and resumes drifting down to make a pile on the floor. How do you get noticed in this swell of paper?

The more professional the appearance of your letter, the better chance you have of getting that coveted call from the production office. But the film industry is also an artistic one, so it's not only important to show that you're a professional but also that you're a professional with flair. Remember that the people who get your letters will take about two seconds to decide if they want to call you or file your resume in the deep dark file cabinet known as the garbage can.

A professional graphics designer who specializes in resumes believes that "you need to communicate that special quality about yourself that will allow the receiver to know who you are," and make you a real person rather than just a piece of paper with a lot of words on it. One way of doing this is by communicating something about your interests. If you love sailing, for example, have a drawing of a catamaran on your letterhead. Or, if you love rock climbing, use a graphic of a rock climber.

Whatever you choose to do, it's important that you be creative, because the people who are looking at your letters appreciate creativity in others. Someone in that production office might like sailing or rock climbing, too. By showing her that you have a common interest you're encouraging her to read your letter and resume, and, hopefully, call you in for an interview.

There are three types of promotional letters that you will use in your efforts to get into the film industry: networking letters, cover letters, and thank-you letters. Using the correct type of letter and format is crucial in creating an effective mailing.

Networking Letters

Networking letters are among the most important you will write during your job search. The purpose of these letters is to approach individuals in the film business for career information, advice, and referrals. They play a key role in your informational interviews, prospecting, and networking activities. Here are some rules to follow when writing a networking letter.

Rule Number 1

Make it professional. Like the resume discussed above, a networking letter is a way to introduce yourself to people in the industry, and you want them to think of you as a professional, even if you aren't one yet. So make sure the letter is clean, clear, and concise, and that there are no typographical errors in it. Also, use a laser printer if you can, and good quality paper.

Rule Number 2

Remember what networking letters are for. These letters are used to gain information, advice, and referrals, not to get a job. You should never say that you're hoping to get a job from the person to whom you're writing. For the same reason, you should also never include your resume, because it sends the wrong message and diminishes the effectiveness of your letter.

Rule Number 3

The most effective networking letters are based on referrals. If you're writing at someone's suggestion, be sure to say so up front. If you don't have a referral, make a logical connection between you and the recipient in your opening paragraph. Try to make this as warm, personal, and professional as possible.

Rule Number 4

Tell the truth. As with the resume—and everything else—it's important that you be completely honest when you approach someone for information and advice.

Rule Number 5

Include an action statement at the end of your letter. Don't expect anyone to call you after receiving your networking letter. You're going to have to make the call, and you should state in the letter when you will do so.

Rule Number 6

Always follow up. If you've said you're going to call, do it, and do it when you said you would.

To follow are two sample networking letters, the first in which the writer has been referred to the recipient and the other in which he has not.

Sample Networking Letter, with Referral

2259 Tall Street
Houston, Texas 32223

September 20, 1999

Chad Stanhope
J.K. Liven Productions
4000 Warner Boulevard
Burbank, California 91522

Dear Mr. Stanhope:

Joanne Smith suggested that I write to you in regard to my
strong interest in being a film editor. Mrs. Smith told me that
you are one of the leading experts in this growing field, and
she thought you would be a good person to give me some
career advice.

I have had two college semesters of experience in video
editing but none thus far in films. I have a particular interest
in special effects and wish to develop my skills in that area.

I will be in southern California next month and am hoping
that it might be possible for us to meet briefly. I am certain
your counsel would be of enormous benefit as I begin looking
for opportunities; I will call your office next week to see if
your schedule permits such a meeting.

Sincerely,

Lauren Borger

Sample Networking Letter, Without Referral

31099 Seventh Avenue
New York, New York 00058

December 29, 1999

Charleen Hechtman
Granada Entertainment
11812 San Vicente Boulevard, Suite 503
Los Angeles, California 90049

Dear Ms. Hechtman:

I am writing to you because I was very impressed with your special effects makeup in the recent film *Werewolf in Paris,* and am interested in meeting with you and learning more about your work.

I have an extensive background in theater makeup and have also worked in film production as a makeup artist, although my experience has been limited to commercials. This experience has led me to decide to begin a career in film as a makeup assistant.

However, before I begin seeking work I feel I must talk to people with makeup experience in films, and I am hoping you can assist me in this regard. I will be in Los Angeles next month and am hoping it might be possible for us to meet briefly. I will call you next week to see if your schedule permits such a meeting.

Sincerely,

Clay Randal Smith

Cover Letters

The cover letter accompanying a resume is the one used most often by people searching for work and serves as your first introduction to a hiring manager or, on a smaller production, the film's producer. The cover letter is read before your resume, and if it's ineffective your resume probably won't even be read.

There are two types of cover letters: targeted and broadcast letters. The targeted letter is more effective and highly recommended over the broadcast letter, because it's addressed to a specific person and refers to a particular position, which may or may not be vacant. Broadcast cover letters are essentially a type of junk mail, and consequently are the least effective in terms of arranging a face-to-face interview.

You will write a targeted letter when you see a specific job listing that includes a specific individual's name, someone refers you to a person whom she knows has an open position, or you research the trades and find a contact on your own. Here are some general rules to follow when you write a targeted letter.

Rule Number 1

Be professional. As with the resume and networking letters, it's important that you present yourself in a professional manner. Make sure that the letter and envelope are neatly typed and free of typographical and grammatical errors. Such errors say a lot about the kind of work you do, so you should have a friend proofread the letter before you send it out.

Rule Number 2

Be brief and to the point. Do not repeat the information on your resume, but draw attention to relevant experience and skills, including the latest film you worked on (once you've done so) and communication and production skills.

Rule Number 3

Always tell the truth about yourself, your experience, and your knowledge of the production company to which you're writing.

Rule Number 4

Indicate what reaction you expect from your letter and how you will follow up.

Rule Number 5

Follow up. If you say you're going to call the letter's recipient—and you should—don't forget to do it.

Rule Number 6

Beware of the dangers of word processing. If you're doing a multiple mailing with mail merge, make sure that you change all the customized statements accordingly. No production company or studio wants to read how much you would like to work for its rival or competitor. Be sure to read each letter before signing it, and make sure that the addressee on the envelope matches the salutation.

Sample Targeted Cover Letter, with Referral

2492 Wannabe Lane
Hollywood, California 90079

July 20, 1999

David Anderson
Shoreline Entertainment
1901 Avenue of the Stars, Suite 1800
Los Angeles, California 90038

Dear Mr. Anderson:

Michael Levy, the artistic director for *Laws of Madness* at Imagine Entertainment, informs me that you have openings for two set painters for your current project, *Match Made in Heaven.*

During the past two years, I've worked as a production assistant and as a set painter on three major motion pictures, as the former during production of *To Have and to Hold,* and as the latter during production of *I'm a Big Boy Now* and *One for the Road.*

I am enclosing my resume for your consideration and would appreciate an opportunity to visit with you and discuss the possibility of being a set painter on *Match Made in Heaven.* I will call you within the next week to make arrangements for a visit.

I look forward to speaking to you.

Sincerely,

Bruce Campbell

Sample Targeted Cover Letter, Without Referral

2189 West Locust Lane
Hollywood, California 90082

July 22, 1999

Patricia Myers
Production Designer
Illusion Entertainment
201 Santa Monica Boulevard, Suite 625
Santa Monica, California 90401

Dear Ms. Myers:

I am writing because I was very impressed with your work on the films *Legends of the Fall* and *Room with a View*. In both films, your designs were particularly effective in recreating a sense of the time in which the films were set, and I would very much like to meet with you and learn more about your work.

My background in film production consists of a year and a half as a production assistant on two films—*Catch Me If You Can* and *Having a Wild Weekend*—during which I was fortunate to work with the set painters. As a result of that experience, I have decided to become a professional set painter.

I would very much like to visit with you and discuss the possibility of working with you in the near future and will call next week to see if your schedule permits such a meeting.

I look forward to meeting with you.

Sincerely,

Rebecca Smith

As mentioned above, broadcast letters are not an effective way of finding work in the film industry. They do, however, work on occasion, and would in any case give you a sense of doing something about your job search without having to go through extensive research to find contact names. More often than not, though, you'll be lucky if you receive one response for every 100 letters you send out.

If you want to try broadcast letters, you should simply write a short three-paragraph cover letter to be sent with your resume. The first two paragraphs introduce you to the employer by discussing your experience, previous performances, and future goals. The final paragraph calls for action on the part of the receiver.

Sample Broadcast Cover Letter

785 Boylston Street
Seattle, Washington 66688

June 28, 1999

Backbreaking Productions
99444 Connastoga Avenue
Los Angeles, California 90099

Attn: Production Office or Unit Production Manager

Over the last several years, I have worked on three local film productions in craft services and as a driver and am hoping within the next year to become a production assistant.

I am particularly interested in taking on new challenges with a film production company that values team performance. As a result of my local experience, I know what it takes to get the job done and am familiar with the long hours and hard work and dedication expected of a production assistant. I love the film business!

I am enclosing a copy of my resume for your consideration. If you have a need for someone with my experience, I would appreciate an opportunity to speak with you about my qualifications and future plans. I may be contacted during the day and evenings at 818-555-2333 and paged at 310-999-2255.

I look forward to hearing from you.

Sincerely,

Seymour Turk

Thank-You Letters

Thank-you letters can be a very effective means of communication when you're searching for a job in the film industry. They demonstrate a notable social grace that says something positive about you as an individual. Even more important, since few individuals take the time to write such letters, those who receive them remember those who do. And one thing you definitely want to do is make sure that people remember you. When someone remembers you, she is much more inclined to furnish you with useful information, advice, and referrals, as well as invite you for job interviews.

In fact, many freelancers in the film industry have discovered that thank-you letters are the most important ones they write.

There are six situations in which it's advisable to send thank-you letters.

Situation Number 1

After receiving information, advice, or a referral from a contact. You should always express your gratitude in writing to contacts who provide you with job search assistance. Not only is it a nice gesture, but individuals who feel appreciated are more likely to remember you and be willing to assist you in the future.

Situation Number 2

Immediately after interviewing for a job. Whether an interview is conducted face-to-face, over the telephone, or on the Internet, you should always write a thank-you letter within 24 hours of the interview. This letter should express your gratitude for the opportunity and reiterate your interest in the job, your career goal, and your major strengths in relation to the employer's needs. All other things being equal, this letter may be the "extra push" that puts you at the top of the employer's list and may very well prove to be the most effective letter in your entire job search.

Situation Number 3

When you want to be withdrawn from further consideration. Sometimes you may decide that you don't want to be considered for a particular position. You may, for example, have been offered a position on another, more desirable production, or decided that the position no longer interests you. For whatever reason, it's important that you don't just cut off the communication. You should write a short thank-you letter informing the company of your withdrawal. You should explain in positive terms why you're no longer interested, and thank them for their time and consideration.

Situation Number 4

After receiving a job offer. Sending a thank-you letter after being hired to work on a film production reconfirms to you and your employer that you are indeed dedicated to the project and look forward to a successful production. Conclude the letter by reaffirming your starting date as well as any other pertinent information, such as shooting locations. Such a thoughtful letter will be well received by the employer and will establish you in his or her mind as an organized and professional individual.

Situation Number 5

On leaving a freelance job. When a film "wraps," a thank-you letter to the director, producer, immediate seniors, and juniors on the crew is a must. You should stress the positive aspect of the working relationship and mention any memorable situations worth sharing.

Situation Number 6

If you've been terminated. Unfortunately, it happens. Although when faced with this situation most people would prefer to have nothing at all to do with their former employers, writing a thank-you note can help to keep your relationship with him or her as cordial as possible. In the letter you should try to be as positive as you can, stressing whatever good things you can about your employment and avoiding mention of anything that could upset your former employer. Since terminated employees almost never write such letters, doing so is likely to create a more positive impression of you in your former employer's mind and make him or her more likely to help you find other jobs or even hire you again.

Sample Thank-You Letter—
Post Informational Interview

3063 West Shore Drive
San Francisco, California 85523

May 29, 1999

Susan Krein
Producer
Top Hat Productions
2259 Wilshire Boulevard, Suite 222
Hollywood, California 90036

Dear Ms. Krein:

I am writing to thank you for giving me the opportunity to meet with you today. As Mr. Jensen had indicated, you are extremely well informed regarding developmental directing, and I appreciate your sharing personal insights with me.

Our discussion was very helpful; I now realize that I would be happier working as a development director for a major studio than on my own as an independent.

You mentioned that you would be happy to put me in contact with several people in your network if I decided this was the direction I wished to take. I would, therefore, appreciate your doing so and will call you in a few days to get these names and addresses from you.

Thank you again for taking the time from your busy schedule to meet with me. I look forward to seeing you again in the future, hopefully when I am working at a major studio as a development director.

Sincerely,

Mandy Plaskett

Sample Thank-You Letter—
Post Job Interview

1958 Clayton Street
Studio City, California 95002

September 26, 1999

Warren Smith
Assistant Producer
Fargo Productions
105 Melrose Avenue
Hollywood, California 90029

Dear Mr. Smith:

I am writing to thank you for the opportunity to interview yesterday for the production assistant position. I very much enjoyed meeting you and the other members of your production team, as well as learning more about your plans for *Rambo VI.*

My interview with you confirmed my initial positive impression of Fargo Productions, and I want to reiterate my strong interest in working for you. I believe that my prior experience as a production assistant would make me a valuable member of your team during the film's production.

Again, thank you for your consideration. If you need any additional information from me, please feel free to call.

Yours truly,

Derrick Stanhope

Sample Thank-You Letter—
Withdrawing from Consideration

2345 Mountain View Road
San Francisco, California 85223

June 13, 1999

Gavin Anderson
Producer
Beatnik Productions
2200 Hollywood Boulevard, Suite 102
Hollywood, California 90027

Dear Mr. Anderson:

I am writing to thank you for giving me the opportunity to interview for the third electrician's position for your production of *Speed 3*. I very much enjoyed meeting you and the other members of the production team and recognize that it would be a privilege for me to work with you.

I must, however, request that you withdraw my name from further consideration for the position, as I have received and accepted an offer to be best boy for Oliver Stone's production of *On Any Sunday*.

I know you will have no trouble finding a competent candidate to fill your opening. When I am done with Mr. Stone's production, I will contact you, and hopefully we will be able to work together at that time.

Sincerely,

Shari Wallace

Sample Thank-You Letter—
Accepting a Job Offer

2589 Jackson Road
Chicago, Illinois 60055

May 15, 1999

Kaila Warren
Personnel Director
Deep Space Nine
Paramount Studios
5555 Melrose Avenue
Los Angeles, California 90038

Dear Ms. Warren:

I want to thank you and Mr. Berman for giving me the opportunity to be a makeup assistant for *Deep Space Nine*. I am very pleased to accept the position and know I'll do a good job for you.

As we discussed, I will begin work on July 6. In the meantime, I'll complete all the necessary employment forms, have the required physical examination, and locate housing. I plan to be in southern California within the next two weeks and would like to deliver the paperwork to you personally, at which time we could discuss any remaining items regarding my employment. I will call next week to schedule an appointment with you.

I enjoyed my interviews with you and Mr. Berman and am looking forward to beginning my job with Paramount Studios.

Sincerely,

Phil Krein

cc: Rick Berman, *Deep Space Nine*

Sample Thank-You Letter— Leaving a Freelance Job

1099 Vermont Avenue
Los Angeles, California 90029

August 12, 1999

Brian Jensen
Editing Department
Warner Bros.
4000 Warner Boulevard, Suite 55
Hollywood, California 90027

Dear Brian:

Now that the production stage of *You Can Take It With You* is over, I just wanted to write to tell you how much I appreciate your having hired me to work on the film and how much I've enjoyed working with you. It's been a very positive experience for me both personally and professionally.

Not only have you been a pleasure to work with, but I also feel that you've taught me a great deal about editing over these last few months, and I want you to know that I very much appreciate it. I sincerely hope that we'll be able to work together again some time in the future.

Sincerely,

Cat Dequire

Sample Thank-You Letter—
On Being Terminated

6656 Norstrand Avenue
Encino, California 90044

July 24, 1999

William Axelrod
Tomorrow Productions
7744 Sepulveda Avenue
Los Angeles, California 90055

Dear Bill:

I am just writing to tell you that, although the circumstances
of my leaving Tomorrow Productions might not have been
the best, I did enjoy working with you and believe that both
the company and I benefited from the two years that I
worked there.

I am now in the process of seeking a new position and will let
you know as soon as I find one. In the meantime, should you
hear of any positions in which you think I might be
interested I'd very much appreciate hearing from you.

Sincerely,

Alan Adail

WRITTEN COMMUNICATIONS CHECKLIST

It's impossible to overemphasize the importance of written communications in finding jobs in the film industry. Because of that, it's important that you follow these general rules in regard to everything you put in writing.

Rule Number 1

> **Make it look professional.** The film industry is full of professionals who pay attention to details. Make sure that all your written communications are printed neatly and cleanly on good-quality paper and are free of typographical or grammatical errors. Proofread it yourself, and have a friend proofread it, too.

Rule Number 2

> **Make it readable.** Be clear and concise in writing your resume and letters. If you have any questions about how clear your writing is, have a friend or friends read it, and listen to them if they have suggestions for changes.

Rule Number 3

> **Always tell the truth.** The film industry is ultimately like a small town—eventually everyone meets everyone else. If you exaggerate your experience or suggest something that isn't true, you will eventually get caught.

Rule Number 4

> **Be creative.** Remember that the film industry is full of creative people who appreciate other creative people. Within limits, it's a good idea to apply that creativity to your letterhead and resume.

Rule Number 5

> **Remember who your reader is.** Different letters serve different purposes. For example, if you're writing a letter requesting a networking interview, be sure not to suggest that you're expecting the recipient to hire you.

Rule Number 6

It's always better to have referrals. People have succeeded without them, but it's always preferable to contact people on the basis of someone else's recommendation. Succeeding in the film business is all about making and keeping contacts, and people are generally happy to share their contacts with you.

Rule Number 7

Always follow up. If you say in a letter that you'll call the recipient next week, make sure you do it. It would even be a good idea to devise some system to keep track of the letters you've written and the follow-up calls you have to make.

Rule Number 8

Write thank-you letters whenever appropriate. Most people don't bother writing thank-you letters even when they should. If you write them both when they're expected and, even more important, when they're not, people will remember you kindly. And remembering you is exactly what you want people to do.

chapter 5

Building and Expanding Your Network

In the film industry, as in life in general, some people seem to have all the luck. Just about everyone knows the story of how Lana Turner was discovered at the Top Hat Cafe across the street from Hollywood High, where she was a student. On that fateful afternoon, she had skipped class and gone to the soda fountain for a Coke when, it so happened, W. R. Wilkerson, the publisher of the *Hollywood Reporter*, walked in. Upon seeing the beautiful girl, Wilkerson approached and asked, "Would you like to be in the movies?"

So, by chance, Lana Turner met the right person who took her to the right parties. At the right party, she met the right producer, who hired her for the right movie. And so began a journey that would eventually lead to fame, fortune, and a place for Lana Turner in Hollywood history.

It does happen, but it happens rarely. Most often, people become stars—or successful behind-the-scenes workers—by moving step-by-step up through the ranks of the industry. And they do it by networking.

The key to networking, of course, is developing contacts. A contact is someone who is interested in you, wants to work with you on a film project, and/or will recommend you to someone who might hire you. Developing those contacts isn't easy, but it can be done.

The film industry is so dependent on freelancers that it requires those involved in it to be constantly networking to find jobs. In fact, if you don't make the effort, chances are you'll never be successful. The key to becoming a successful behind-the-scenes worker is to build a strong foundation of contacts and to make those contacts early through proper networking.

WHOM TO CONTACT AND HOW TO FIND THEM

The only way you're going to establish a network of individuals to help you find work in the film industry is to get out there and look. First you need to know whom to contact. Potential contacts fall into three groups: people inside the industry, people in industry organizations, and people outside the industry.

People Inside the Industry

For obvious reasons, people inside the industry are those you'd most like to have as contacts, particularly those at the top of the business, like producers and directors. There's no reason not to try starting at the top. If you're in a small town, call the chamber of commerce and ask if there are any local film studios. If you're near a major city, get in touch with a motion picture studio. You can even look in the yellow pages under Motion Pictures—Production Companies. If you can get in to see one of these people, you're ahead of the game.

However, don't neglect potential contacts at lower levels. Contacts lead to other contacts, and sometimes one of those people in the electrical, grip, art, or editorial departments can lead you to someone higher up who is in a position to offer you a job.

People in Industry Organizations

Involving yourself in one way or another with film-related organizations is an excellent way of meeting people. One of the best ways to develop contacts is to work on a project by joining an industry or professional trade association, such as Women In Film, Northern California Writers and Artists, Independent Feature Producers West, or International Documentary Association. It's a very good networking device, not only because you can meet lots of people, but also because there's an inherent tendency to hire "one's own." If you're a member of the family, so to speak, you've got a better chance of landing a job. You might also want to volunteer for the American Film Institute. It's not only a great cause—the preservation of our film heritage—but a great way to meet professionals in the field.

You should also check with the guild or union that represents people in the field you're interested in joining. Most guilds and unions have Web sites, which contain ample data on how to contact industry professionals. Here are some of the major ones.

The Motion Picture Editors Guild
http://www.cyberfilmschool.com/main.htm
7715 Sunset Boulevard
Suite 200
Hollywood, CA 90046
Phone 213-876-4770 Fax 213-876-0861

—has a very useful Web site that provides suggestions on starting out in the field of editing

American Society of Cinematographers (ASC)
http://www.cinematographer.com

—has links to mailing lists and resources for jobs and information on becoming a member

The International Alliance of Theatrical Stage Employees, Moving Picture Technicians, Artists and Allied Crafts of the United States and Canada (IATSE)
http://www.iatse.lm.com

—provides information on how to join the union and connects you to local branches around the world; contact your local branch and make industry contacts through them

Directors Guild of America (DGA)
http://www.dga.org
7920 Sunset Boulevard
Los Angeles, CA 90046
Phone 310-289-2000   Fax 310-289-2029

—in addition to other information, tells you how to get into its mentoring program; there are DGA offices in New York, Chicago, and Florida

Producers Guild of America
http://producersguild.com/contents.html
—has a very informative Web site that contains a great deal of information on how to produce feature films

Society of Motion Picture and Television Engineers (SMPTE)
http://www.smpte.org
595 W. Hartsdale Avenue
White Plains, NY 10607
Phone 914-761-1100   Fax 914-761-3115

—the preeminent professional society for motion picture and television engineers, with approximately 10,000 members worldwide

Academy of Motion Picture Arts and Sciences
http://www.ampas.org
8949 Wilshire Boulevard
Beverly Hills, CA 90211
Phone 310-247-3000   Fax 310-859-9351 or 310-859-9619

—a wonderful Web site that provides information on fellowships, the Academy library, and special events at which you can contact movers and shakers

International Documentary Association
http://www.documentary.org
1551 South Robertson Boulevard
Suite 201
Los Angeles, CA 90035-4257
Phone 310-284-8422   Fax 310-785-9334

—a nonprofit association whose purpose is to support the efforts of documentary film and video makers around the world; its members include producers, directors, writers, editors, camera operators, musicians, researchers, technicians, journalists, broadcast and cable executives, academics, distributors, and members of the general public

American Film Institute
http://www.afionline.org
2021 North Western Avenue
Los Angeles, CA 90027
Phone 213-856-7600   Fax 213-467-4578

—a particularly useful Web site with information on workshops, seminars, classes, and job listings

Hollywood Creative Directory
http://www.hcdonline.com
3000 West Olympic Boulevard
Suite 2525
Santa Monica, CA 90404
Phone (within California) 310-315-4815
Phone (outside California) 800-815-0503
Fax 310-315-4816

—gives you the opportunity to review and purchase its many film and television guides, which cover everything from agents and managers to producers and distributors

L.A. 411 Online
http://www.LA411.com

—provides you with immediate access to 13,000 professional industry resources within 226 categories, each listing having been carefully researched and qualified by its editorial team; can list your services on this Web site or search for contacts for networking (Their book, *L.A. 411*, has been used as a guide to film industry professionals for nearly two decades. It costs $68 and can be purchased through the Web site or by phone at 800-545-2411.)

Finally, you can take classes and attend workshops offered by universities, film schools, or Learning Annexes. These are great ways to meet similarly minded people. You can usually find 2 to 5 people to exchange cards with and start a correspondence. Pamela Jaye Smith, a film consultant, director, and producer, is now working on a couple of projects with a woman she met years ago at a UCLA seminar.

People Outside the Industry

Don't forget about all the people you know who aren't in Hollywood or the film business. You never know who might lead to someone—or something— exciting, so get in touch with people you know, tell them you're interested in getting into films, and ask them if they can suggest anyone to contact. Call everyone you know—friends, relatives, in-laws, neighbors, old acquaintances. They may have a cousin or a friend who's a producer or screenwriter, and they'd probably be delighted to recommend you to "their friend in Hollywood."

This is the way that Helen got into the business. She had a wonderful script and a friend who wasn't in the industry but happened to know a producer. Her friend got the script to the producer, the film was made, and everyone was happy. Of course, both Helen and the producer appreciated their mutual friend bringing them together and turned to her later when they were seeking further contacts.

While connections like this don't always turn out as well, when it comes to the film industry, contacts can come from the most surprising places. Naturally, the more people you connect with (whether it's a script person, a hairdresser, or a taxi driver), the better off you'll be.

WHAT TO DO ONCE YOU'VE FOUND THEM

Now that you've found a potential contact, you can just call, write, or walk into his or her office and ask for a job, right? Wrong!

Asking someone to give you a job or to get you a job will almost always end a conversation quickly. That's not what networking is about.

What it is about is building up a group of contacts who will, hopefully, one day lead you to someone who's actually making a film and looking for someone with your abilities. It's a slow, sometimes tedious, and often frustrating process, but it's also essential. If you approach it the right way, it can also be an enjoyable experience. Not only will you be able to talk about something you love with people who feel the same way you do, but chances are you'll also meet some pretty fascinating people, some of whom may become close friends and colleagues you'll value for years to come. The key is to have a well thought-out plan so you can build a strong foundation of contacts who will help you get work now and continue to help you in the future.

During this phase of your job search, you will want to set up two kinds of interviews: informational interviews and networking interviews. While the preparation and planning for both are similar, their purposes are different.

You'll want to set up informational interviews if you're unsure of what area of film production you're interested in or if you have an idea of the field but don't know very much about it. Informational interviews are a way of gaining knowledge of the field by speaking with an authoritative and dependable source. They give you a look at people who are doing what you think you want to do and allow you to investigate the diversity of specialties in any given choice in the film business. If you think you may be interested in becoming a set painter, for example, talking to someone who is working as a set painter is an excellent way to find out exactly what kind of work he or she does and to see if this is really something you would like to do.

Informational interviews, however, are not job interviews. At this point all you're doing is preparing for the initial interview with someone who is looking for someone in your chosen field. You're just collecting information that will help you in your quest to be successful in the film industry. If the people you're meeting discover that you're trying to use the opportunity to get a job and not just to find out what the job is like, they will be very upset because you were not up front with them. You are there to learn, not to promote yourself

Once you've decided what you want to do in the film industry and learned whatever you can about your chosen field, the next step is to arrange networking interviews. The purpose of networking interviews is not directly to get a job but to start making contacts that will eventually lead you to someone who is actually hiring people. The people you meet at such interviews may or may not have openings, but if they don't they will in all likelihood be able to lead you, eventually, to people who do.

Regardless of the kind of interview you want to arrange, the first step is making contact, and that process is always the same.

How to Make Contact

If you're feeling nervous about making that first contact, it's a good idea to remember that, as a rule, people in the film business like to help other people. At some point in the past someone helped them get into the industry, and they like to return the favor.

When it comes to networking, there are several ways to contact people: by accosting them somewhere (e.g., a restaurant), by calling them on the phone, or by writing them a letter. Accosting them is definitely not a good idea—it virtually never works. Of the other two methods, using the phone is a more direct, more immediate, and to some extent more personal way. However, contacting people in writing—by mail, e-mail, or fax—also has some advantages. Incidentally, it would be a good idea for you to familiarize yourself with the latest technology. People seeking jobs in the film industry via faxes, commercial and personal Web sites, and e-mail tend to communicate a higher level of competence to employers.

Whether you're calling or writing, it's always preferable to be able to say that someone suggested you contact the person you're trying to reach. If you have a friend, for example, who knows the heads of production at a couple of Hollywood studios, you can call or write them, mentioning up front that "so-and-so" suggested you contact them. People are more likely to pay attention if you've been referred to them by someone they know.

Regardless of how you decide to contact people, it's important to remember that the goal of this initial contact is to get an interview, not a job—at least not right now. In fact, for an informational interview, you should specifically say that you are only looking for information. For a networking interview, you should say that you don't expect the person to necessarily have a job opening at the moment. What you're trying to do at this point is give the people you're contacting enough information to enable them to decide whether to meet with you and/or provide you with additional networking contacts.

Telephone Scripts

If you're going to make contact by telephone, you'll need a telephone script, which is essentially a condensed version of your resume. The script should cover your strongest skills and best personal traits and should follow a pattern: education first, followed by hard skills, soft skills, and personality traits.

The script should take no more than 40 seconds to present, because if you go on for too long the person on the other end of the phone is going to tune you out. You don't have to rush—you can say a lot in 40 seconds. It's also important that, even though you may actually be reading the script, it doesn't sound like you are. For that reason, it's a good idea to practice saying your script to a wall until you feel comfortable using it and then trying it out on a friend. By practicing the script, you'll develop a conversational tone and improve the timing of your delivery.

When you're delivering your script, you should be friendly and confident. This is your opportunity to demonstrate your professionalism and your ability to communicate. If you hesitate or sound unsure of yourself, the person you're calling will interrupt your presentation. Here's a sample script for someone who doesn't have any work experience and wants to arrange a networking interview:

- Hello, is this _____?

- My name is Jane Jobseeker, and I'm calling at the suggestion of _____.

- I've been studying filmmaking for the last few years and hoping to get into the field as a production assistant.

- I have wonderful people skills, and I love to work hard.

- As a team member, I can help start things and finish them.

- I'm energetic, punctual, and can be counted on in a pinch to work overtime.

- I don't expect you to have a job available at the moment, but I'm hoping that we might be able to get together to discuss my skills and abilities further.

- Would you have some time to see me this week or next? What would be convenient for you?

Of course, not everyone will agree to see you. In that case, ask if the person could suggest someone else you might talk to. In any case, it's important that you be gracious, even if you're turned down for an interview. Chances are, once you do get into the business, you'll run across these people again, and you don't want them to remember you as that nasty young person who took rejection poorly.

Letters

Some people have problems with calling people they don't know, and if you're one of them, making contact in writing may be a better way to go. If you write first and follow up with a phone call, you'll know that the person on the other end of the line has at least some idea of who you are.

If you choose this method, you'll have to put together a networking letter to send along with your resume, as discussed in the previous chapter. A networking letter should contain the same basic information as a telephone script. If you're writing at someone's suggestion, you should say so up front and tell the person that you're writing to seek their advice and counsel. You should explain that you're interested in getting into the film industry and provide some information about your education, skills, and personal traits. Finally, you should ask the person to meet with you briefly and promise to call soon to set up an appointment.

Chances are that if you send out ten networking letters, you'll wind up getting a job, although probably not directly from any of those ten people. Remember, one contact always leads to others, and the more people who know you're looking for a job, the more likely you are to get one.

As mentioned above, it's best if you can say someone suggested you contact the person you're writing to, but you can also do cold mailings of your resume, along with your networking letter, to companies in the *L.A. 411* directory for commercials, the *Hollywood Creative Directory* for features and TV, and members of the International Documentary Association for documentaries. Be sure to address the letters to specific individuals, because otherwise they're likely to wind up in the circular file. This cold-call method once landed Pamela Jaye Smith not only a long-term freelance job with a commercial production company, but also a good colleague and dear friend (we'll talk about Pamela's story later in this chapter).

Remember, too, that when you're writing cover letters or making phone calls it's important to keep thorough notes and have a calendar on hand to write down mailings, appointments, and callback dates and times. The more organized you are, the easier it will be for you to follow up and not lose your contacts.

How to Have a Successful Meeting

Congratulations! You've scheduled a meeting. Now you need to prepare yourself for it. It's advisable to find out as much about the person you're meeting as possible. This should be relatively easy, as there's ample data available on production companies—some even have their own Web sites. The resources mentioned in the "Organizations" section of this chapter will also help you with your research.

Interviews can last anywhere from 10 minutes to 3 hours. Usually, they're closer to 10 minutes because people in film production companies are very busy. Even if you made initial contact with the person in writing, be sure to bring extra resumes to the meeting. Remember, this is your opportunity to shine—to convince someone in the business that you have what it takes to make it.

Preparing for the Meeting

Before you even step out of your door to go to a meeting, regardless of what kind of meeting it is, it's necessary that you prepare yourself. Again, while there are similarities between informational and networking interviews, there are also several differences. In either case, it's important to prepare yourself both mentally and physically.

You should start by practicing your interview skills with someone whom you know will not hold back and doesn't mind telling you that you need more practice. This could be a parent, a brother or sister, a friend, a teacher, or a neighbor. Have the person give you feedback on how well you perform. For example: Is your voice clear and understandable? Do you look comfortable? Do you make good eye contact?

You might also want to videotape yourself in an interview situation. Watching yourself on tape may be embarrassing, but it can be a great way to find out what you do well and what areas you could improve on. Seeing yourself on tape will enable you to notice any odd habits you have, such as fidgeting, giggling nervously, or slouching, that you need to work on.

People in the film industry usually do not dress formally. To find your dress code, check out the top players in your chosen position. There are different looks for different jobs. Studio producers and agents don't look like cinematographers or gaffers.

The jobs in Hollywood are creative. The aim is to look expensive while wearing play clothes. It is casual yet expensive and hip. The key to dress is to stay in the spirit of the time.

What about traditional wear? When someone in a suit and tie walks onto a set, there are murmurs of "Heads up. There are suits on the set." It is not a complimentary term. However, many creative executives and most business executives, agents, lawyers, and accountants wear suits.

Pay attention to the accepted dress of the top people in your chosen position. However, it is also beneficial to develop a look that is all your own. You will then stand out from the crowd, and people will remember you. Personal image consultants in the film industry or costume designers can help you with this, because you certainly would not want your "new" look to backfire.

You should also take care of your personal hygiene. Remember to wear antiperspirant, shave, have clean hair, and avoid trendy makeup and jewelry.

Before going to a meeting, prepare a brief statement, similar to a telephone script, explaining who you are, what you want to be, and why you wanted to see this person. Be prepared to express your strong desire to be whatever it is you want to be in the film industry, if you know. People in film, as in other industries, are impressed with newcomers who have a clear idea of what they want to do.

For an informational interview, you'll also want to devise a series of questions to ask. The idea here is to ask about those things that are important to you and to let the conversation flow naturally while making sure you get the information you need. It's best to stick to the topic of the meeting. You only have so much time, and you do not want to lose the opportunity to find out everything you can about the profession.

The kind of questions you might ask include:

- How did you choose this field of the film industry?
- How did you get into this field?
- What do you like best about your work?
- What do you like the least?
- What kind of skills, education, and/or training would I need to get into this area?
- What do you consider your major accomplishments?
- Were there any unusual difficulties you had to overcome in achieving these accomplishments?

- What two or three things do you feel you have learned on this job?
- What are some examples of important types of decisions or recommendations you're called upon to make?
- How do you go about making these decisions or recommendations?
- What decisions are easiest for you to make and which ones are more difficult?
- What were some of the things you did that helped you to advance in the film industry?
- Who were some of the people you feel helped you and why was their help so beneficial to you?
- What is a typical entry-level salary? (Do not ask how much the person you are interviewing makes now!)
- What are your aspirations for the future? Have these changed in the last five years? If so, how and why?
- If you were to start over, what would you do now to get your career in film established?
- Is there anyone else you think I should talk to who's doing this kind of work?

Because you're not specifically looking for information during a networking interview, it's not necessary for you to devise as many questions—three or four industry-related questions should be sufficient. Here's where your research will come in handy. If, for example, you're meeting with a set designer who's about to start work on a period film, you might ask about the particular challenges she expects to face. Or, if you're meeting with a cinematographer and you know that Kodak just came out with a special new lens for use in films, you might ask him how he thinks it will affect the craft. Remember that people in films love to talk about what they do and will be flattered to be asked their opinions.

The Meeting

The first 5 minutes of an interview—informational, networking, or otherwise—set the tone for the rest of the interview. If you can make a good impression and maintain a relaxed attitude from the outset, you will find that the rest of the interview will roll right along. Here are some helpful suggestions that should ensure the interview gets off on the right foot.

- Greet the interviewer. It sounds simple, but many people forget this basic courtesy.
- Smile. A sincere smile can do a lot to put both of you at ease.
- Introduce yourself. Don't assume the interviewer already knows your name.
- Shake hands firmly and warmly.
- Make eye contact when speaking, but don't stare the interviewer down. Maintain eye contact the way that you would with a friend during a casual conversation.
- Stand until the interviewer asks you to sit down.
- Relax and sit naturally but don't slump in your chair or lean on the interviewer's desk.
- Be prepared to make small talk to put both of you at ease. If you are familiar with his or her work in film, mention this in a complementary way, but don't overdo it.
- Be prepared to talk about yourself as a person.
- Speak in a firm, clear, and confident voice. You may have great answers to the interviewer's questions, but that won't matter if your responses are so muffled or timidly expressed that the interviewer cannot hear you or does not believe you.
- Maintain a positive attitude through the interview.
- Don't overstay your welcome. When you feel the conversation is beginning to wind down, tell the person that you know how busy he or she is and that you don't want to take up any more time.
- Always ask if there are any other people whom you should contact and whether or not it's all right for you to use the interviewer's name.
- Before you leave, be sure to thank the person for the time he or she has spent with you.

Don't even think about being offered a job, particularly in an informational interview. A networking interview might result in an offer, but don't expect it to. If you've made a good impression, the person will remember you and may contact you with a job offer in the future. The important thing is that you had the opportunity to talk to someone in the industry, and if you keep at it long enough, eventually that job offer will come.

The Rules of Networking
There are certain rules in networking that you should follow whether you're just starting out or have been in the business for years.

Rule Number 1
Always tell the truth. Don't lie about your experience or your ability. It's easy for people to find out if and where you've worked before, and if they discover that you've lied they won't think too kindly of you.

Rule Number 2
Don't ask for too much too soon. This can sometimes prevent a contact from wanting to hire you or give you a referral. Don't expect the million-dollar job yet—you have to work your way up the ranks. Be grateful that someone is willing to take your name and number.

Rule Number 3
Listen. So often neophytes are so busy promoting themselves that they don't give the contact a chance to answer their questions or offer advice. Once you've had your say, make sure to let your contact talk.

Rule Number 4
Be professional. First impressions really do matter. Always act and dress in the manner of your chosen profession, even—or especially—if you're not actually in that profession yet.

Following Up

Following up on meetings is extremely important. You should always send thank-you notes to your contacts within a day or two of the interviews. In these notes you should thank them again for seeing you, remind them—nicely—of any specific assistance they may have offered to provide, mention any additional action you would like them to take, and tell them what actions, if any, you plan to take. You should also tell them that you'll stay in touch and keep them posted on your career. If your new contact suggested other people to get in touch with, call or write them as soon as possible and set up appointments.

KEEPING IN TOUCH WITH YOUR CONTACTS

You should have a short-term (four to six weeks) and long-term (three or more months) contact list. Call your best contacts every four to six weeks just to stay in touch. A quick "Hi, what's up?" will not be an imposition on them. You should also ask when it would be a good time to ring back, in a month or two, or whatever.

Another way of keeping in touch with your best contacts is to send revised resumes or newsy little letters about what you've been up to—latest jobs, etc. Postcards with news of significant career steps are also good. Kelly's story is a good example of how keeping in touch with contacts can pay off.

Kelly was 19 when she first came to Los Angeles to find a job in the industry. Although her first love was acting, she felt she'd be happy with any type of work in the business. Her first job was as a runner for an agency. She would bring the agency's submissions to casting directors in town, often sneaking her own pictures and resume into the bundle. Having thus met quite a few casting directors, she decided that she'd stay in touch with a little help from Hallmark.

On every holiday under the sun she would send out Charlie Brown/Peanuts cards, the purpose being to create a theme associated with her name to keep herself fresh in these people's minds. It paid off, with two television acting jobs and a good shot at a feature film. Her first job came from a casting director who said, laughing, that he'd hire her as long as she promised to not send anymore Charlie Brown cards.

Due to the nature of the film industry, you can never tell when one of those contacts you made will result in a job. Pamela Jaye Smith's story is a good example.

For more than twenty years, Pamela has worked as a consultant, producer, writer, and director of features, television shows, commercials, documentaries, and corporate films. She also consults with organizations and individuals who want to redesign themselves, their images, and/or their careers. "When I moved to Hollywood," she says, "I got a job the first day I went looking and spent six weeks at a script-typing service, which was great to learn format and see who was doing what in stories."

Then she tracked down some contacts she had made while working on a film for Paramount Pictures in her home state of Texas. "I had the good fortune of getting a job with a new production company headed by someone I'd met there on location. So networking was everything there. . . . On my own, I applied for and got work at Universal Studios, where I was in production for four years on TV series, movies of the week, and features. Contacts from those years have lasted for a very long time, and I still do business with some of the same people as we've all moved along in our careers. Some are among my very best friends and we consider each other family."

Always remember people who have helped you along the way. These people are special. They didn't have to take time from their work to show you the ropes. They did it because they liked and respected you. And never forget that you are a member of a team. No one can make a film alone—it takes hundreds of dedicated people.

HOW TO MAKE SURE THEY CAN FIND YOU

Unless you are a wealthy recluse or a serial killer, make sure you are easy to find. The worst thing that can happen is that someone wants to hire you for a job or has heard about a job you'd be interested in but can't contact you because she doesn't know where to reach you.

You should, of course, be listed in the phone book. People can lose your number, but as long as they remember your name they'll be able to find you.

You should have business cards and resumes to give out to people you meet and, if appropriate, include with any letters or gifts you may send. Make sure the cards have every phone and fax number at which people can reach you, as well as your e-mail address. You also need to have a pager and/or voice mail service.

When you meet people and they ask you for your business card, make a brief note on your card about where and when you met them and the subject of your discussion. That way, when they go through their wallet or purse a week later, they will remember you. Don't forget to get their business card so you will know how to reach them.

If you want to be in the film business, you should be registered in directories, film commission handbooks, and association membership guides, some of which are listed in the "Organizations" section of this chapter. For example, there's a Northern California Film and Television Directory called "The Source," so if you want to work in this area you should purchase a listing or a display ad in this directory.

NETWORKING CHECKLIST

Networking is an ongoing process, something that never stops as long as you're in the film industry, but this list will serve as a way to get yourself organized and start networking.

1. Make separate lists of all the people you know and/or would like to know in the industry, all the appropriate organizations you should contact, and all the people you know outside the industry. This will be the beginning of your contact list.

2. Create a form or devise some other method for keeping track of whom you've contacted and the outcome of each phone conversation or interview.

3. If you're going to make contact by phone, write and study your telephone script and practice it before you call.

4. If you're going to make contact in writing, write a model networking letter you can adapt to whomever you're sending it to. Be sure to update it as appropriate. Remember to include your resume with every letter, e-mail, or fax you send out.

5. Prepare for every meeting by learning as much about the person you'll be seeing as you can, preparing a brief explanation of why you wanted to meet, and creating a series of appropriate questions.

6. Act at all times during a meeting in a polite and professional but friendly manner. Dress for the position you want. Look your contact in the eye when you speak.

7. Don't forget to ask about other people to contact, making sure you can use your contact's name.

8. Always write a follow-up thank-you letter within a day or two of your meeting.

9. Follow up by contacting anyone else the person you've met with has suggested.

10. Keep in touch with your contacts on a regular basis.

chapter 6

Join a Group, Take a Seminar, or Attend a Festival

Like every industry, the film industry has its own organizations and associations, and joining one or more of them is an extremely effective way of meeting people who may ultimately want to hire you. You need to make it your business to know about the most important groups, and join at least one that appears to offer a way to network with appropriate contacts in the industry.

The Academy of Motion Picture Arts and Sciences and the Academy of Television Arts and Sciences are obvious choices, and both are very good groups to join because they offer numerous benefits and opportunities. You might also, for example, be interested in Women In Film or the Independent Feature Project. The American Film Institute is an excellent organization, as is the International Documentary Association, which is home to many nonfiction film and television producers. You might even want to join the guild or union that represents people in your field of interest.

No matter what group you decide to be a part of, simply joining isn't enough. The important thing is to get involved. You should become active on a committee, work on a project, or run for office. Remember that the boards of directors and staffs of these organizations are important, respected, well-connected people in the film community, and getting to know them as working colleagues can be of inestimable value to your career.

Once you have targeted a few organizations that interest you, call and ask for membership information and a current calendar. Then, if you like what you read, you should attend an event. If membership fees are out of your reach at the moment, you can sometimes attend expensive fund-raisers or seminars for free if you're willing to work at the event, or you can volunteer to help in the office or on a committee.

There are also many seminars and classes given on various aspects of the industry. Just about every guild and association holds seminars, and many educational institutions offer them as well. Most are presented in New York, Los Angeles, and San Francisco, and virtually all of them are open to the public.

In addition to the obvious learning opportunities offered by seminars or classes, there are other ways you can benefit from attending them. They give you the opportunity to network and to get to know people who normally might not return your calls. Many top industry players speak at these meetings, and it's possible for you to approach them during breaks or after classes. This is a relaxed atmosphere in which it's sometimes easier to make a contact, which you can follow up later with calls or letters.

You can also use these meetings to create your own networking group. You might, for example, take an industry seminar in your area of interest—such as writing, make-up, or editing. At the meeting you can pass around a notepad and collect names and addresses of fellow students. Afterwards, pick a bar or restaurant and send out invitations to a no-host networking party, so people can keep in touch and share information about jobs.

Alternatively, you could start your own group with selected industry friends. Lew Hunter, a screenwriter and teacher of screenwriting at UCLA, and his wife formed such a group, which they call Writer's Block. Lew and his wife hold a party periodically at their house, which is attended by students and former students who pay a nominal fee or bring their own food and drink. Lew and his wife love it because it enables them to stay in touch with his students, and it provides the students with a great opportunity to network with top industry players.

Finally, there are a number of film festivals and conventions you can attend, such as the annual Sundance Film Festival in Park

City, Utah. The nearby ski slopes at Sundance are a great place to meet people and network, particularly because they offer a more relaxed, informal setting than the usual frenetic Hollywood venues. People who don't call you back in Hollywood will be happy to talk to you on a lift to the next ski run or after an excellent day of skiing.

ORGANIZATIONS AND ASSOCIATIONS

Here are some of the key groups you should explore to help you break into a film career.

The Academy of Motion Picture Arts and Sciences (AMPAS)

encourages filmmakers and students toward successful careers.

8949 Wilshire Boulevard
Beverly Hills, CA 90211
Phone: 310-247-3000
Fax: 310-859-9351 or 310-859-9619
E-mail: ampas@oscars.org
Web site: http://www.ampas.org

Contact: Linda Harris Mehr
Founded: 1929; Open: 9 a.m. to 5 p.m. Monday through Friday; Cost: N/A; Job Placement: N/A.

The Academy of Motion Picture Arts and Sciences is, of course, best known for its annual awards ceremony, but the academy also offers the Margaret Herrick Library as the world's most extensive and comprehensive research and reference library, containing materials documenting both an art form and an industry.

The Academy of Television Arts & Sciences (ATAS)
offers repertory groups for actors, directors, and writers.

5220 Lankeeshim Boulevard
North Hollywood, CA 91601
Phone: 818-754-2800
Fax: 818-761-2827
E-mail: facultyseminar@emmys.org
Web site: http://www.emmy.org

Contact: Ms. Price Hicks
Founded 1946; Open: Monday through Friday 8:30 a.m. to
5:30 p.m.; Cost: $25–$125; Job Placement: Yes.

The Academy of Television Arts and Sciences offers useful
seminars and panel discussions.

Women In Film (WIF)
is for women professionals, including producers, directors,
writers, technical crew, artists, and freelancers.

6464 Sunset Boulevard
Suite 530
Hollywood, CA 90028
Phone: 213-463-6040
Fax: 213-463-0963
E-mail: wifla@aol.com
Web site: http://www.wif.org

Contact: Bobbie Frank, Special Events Producer
Founded: 1973; Open: Year-round; Cost: Membership Dues
$125/year; Job Placement: Yes.

Women In Film was founded in Los Angeles to "recognize,
develop, and actively promote the unique visions of women in
the global communications industry." Today, WIF has more
than 2,500 members in the greater Los Angeles area, with
thirty autonomous national and international chapters that
have an additional 10,000 members. It's the foremost
organization for women in the entertainment industry.

WIF is an advocate of equal opportunity and fair employment practices, and its goals include working for the full integration of women into industry positions of authority and visibility and the more positive depiction of women in the media. Not surprisingly, much of WIF's work revolves around educating and training women to step into frontline positions and producing their own films.

Contact WIF in Los Angeles if you're interested in joining one of the chapters. If you're a woman living in southern California, you may want to look into WIF's workshops on directing, pitching, producing, and screenwriting. WIF also offers seminars and panel discussions on topics such as financial management and working with agents. The organization also provides opportunities to learn the ropes from other women through mentoring and internship programs, networking breakfasts and luncheons, industry mixers, and other events.

Independent Feature Project (IFP)/West
is for emerging and established independent feature filmmakers, producers, directors, screenwriters, and other film professionals.

1625 Olympia Boulevard
Santa Monica, CA 90404
Phone: 310-392-8832 or 800-471-4437
Fax: 310-392-6792
E-mail: ifpw@aol.com
Web Site: http://www.ipwest.org

Contact: Jennifer Schems, Director of Membership
Founded: 1981; Open: Year-round; Cost: Membership Dues $85/year; Job Placement: Yes.

IFP was originally founded in New York and still maintains an office there (see separate listing below), but the West Coast group, with a membership of more than 3,500, has emerged as its own organization. There is still, however, cooperation between the two groups—they jointly publish the indispensable quarterly *Filmmaker*—and among other IFP chapters.

IFP/West is best known nationally for its Independent Spirit Awards, the self-proclaimed "premiere annual event in the independent film community," but the organization also offers year-round educational programs and sneak previews of next season's independent hits.

Among the programs IFP/West offers is "The Producer Series," panel discussions with independent filmmakers who have been there, done that, and survived to share their war stories and survival tips. Another program, the "Master Workshops," offers a wide variety of sessions on everything from sound design for guerrilla filmmakers to insider panels on how to work the press before your feature is released. Look for the "Evening With . . ." series to meet the likes of Jodie Foster, Robert Altman, or Quentin Tarantino. Plan your calendar around the "Breakfast Series" to meet talent and literary agents in an intimate setting and the "Spotlight Luncheons" with top executives from such companies as New Line, Gramercy, Miramax, and Trimark. A note to the not-so-well-to-do: IFP/West has a tradition of reserving for each of its events a handful of $1 tickets for members only, first come, first served, at the door.

The American Film Institute (AFI)
is for dramatic and narrative filmmakers and industry professionals and also offers public programs.

2201 North Western Avenue
Los Angeles, CA 90027
Phone: 213-856-7600
Fax: 213-467-4578
Web site: http://www.afionline.org

Contact: Professional Training Division
Founded: 1967; Open: September–June; Cost: Admission application $75, resume, letter, sample work, and recommendation (optional); Job Placement: Yes.

For professional training, registration forms and fee deadlines: early January for CAFTS; ongoing for Professional Training, $30–$600 per class or series; Financial Aid: loans and scholarships; Degree or Certification: M.F.A. or nondegree Certificate of Attendance in Cinematography, Directing, Editing, Producing, Production Design, Screenwriting, and Digital Media.

The main thrust of the American Film Institute's Education and Training Programs is its Center for Advanced Film and Television Studies (CAFTS), a highly competitive and prestigious two-year graduate program founded in 1969 for "today's most promising filmmakers." In a departure from traditional academic programs, CAFTS was patterned after European conservatories, in which talented individuals study with leading artists.

The emphasis is on feature films with character-driven screenplays. Fellows in the First Year Program collaborate to create a short narrative project, with student teams drawn from six program disciplines: cinematography, directing, editing, producing, production design, and screenwriting (the newest discipline, digital media, is in the works). Courses within each discipline are supplemented by master seminars. This is a full-time program, so you won't be able to hold down a job or take classes elsewhere during the first year. Also, the program is so intense that it won't leave you any free time. Fellows nominated for and accepted into the Second Year Program are funneled into similar collaborative Production, Resident, or Screenwriting programs.

Second Year Fellows who already hold a B.A. degree, complete the program, and receive approval after a faculty review of their work receive an M.F.A. degree. Those who enter without a B.A. are called Associate Fellows and receive a Certificate of Attendance instead of an M.F.A. degree.

If you're not interested in the full academic program, you should look into the public programs offered through AFI's Professional Training Division. Its Film and Television Arts Program features seminars, lectures, and workshops for the novice or professional, and its Advanced Technology Program offers a lab for hands-on training and experimentation on state-of-the-art computer workstations. AFI's national workshops, such as the Directing Workshop for Women and Television Writers Summer Workshop, limit their enrollment by competitive applications.

AFI is an excellent place to learn your craft and make contacts, as it is closely connected to the film industry. Its distinguished roster of alumni includes, among others, directors Mimi Leder (*Deep Impact*) and Amy Heckerling (*Clueless*), cinematographers Janusz Kaminksi (*Schindler's List*) and Amir Mokri (*Pacific Heights*), and screenwriters Paul Schrader and Susannah Grant (*Pocahontas*). AFI is among the country's top graduate film schools, as are New York University, the University of Southern California, and the University of California at Los Angeles.

Film Arts Foundation (FAF)
is for independent film and videomakers.

346 Ninth Street
2nd Floor
San Francisco, CA 94103
Phone: 415-552-8760
Fax: 415-552-0882
Web site: http://www.sirius.com/~sstark/org/faf/faf.html

Contact: Danny Plotnick, Seminar Coordinator
Founded: 1976; Open: Year-round; Cost: $5–$375 per class or series; Job Placement: Yes.

In the heart of San Francisco's artist-heavy South of Market neighborhood, the Film Arts Foundation is a regional service organization with a national profile. Founded by a handful of filmmakers, FAF now has about 3,500 members working in film, video, and multimedia and is the largest regional organization of its kind in the country. Members range from first-timers and students to internationally acclaimed filmmakers.

FAF provides a full range of year-round services to independent film and videomakers with its annual Film Arts Festival, monthly magazine *Release Print*, yearly grants to area artists, brimming resource library, and fiscal sponsorship. Outside of film schools, FAF operates the most extensive nonprofit film facility (cameras, Nagra and DAT recorders, flatbeds, and optical printer) west of the Mississippi and has recently added an Avid nonlinear editing system.

FAF's monthly lineup of evening and weekend classes includes everything from hands-on technical workshops to business, fundraising, and legal seminars to occasional town hall meetings on subjects such as "Truth in the Documentary." In a lecture series with maverick filmmakers and standard-bearers of the American independent feature film movement, you'll find such people as Frederick Wiseman, Albert Maysles, James Schamus, John Pierson, Barbara Trent, and Christine Vachon. Considering everything offered, FAF classes have emerged as an intriguing and affordable alternative to film school.

San Francisco has, in fact, become a film center in its own right. The Ninth Street Media Arts building, which contains the Film Arts Foundation, also contains the headquarters of the National Asian American Telecommunications Association, Cine Accion, Frameline, the Jewish Film Festival, and the National Alliance for Media Arts and Culture. In a bold cross-cultural experiment, six of the country's leading media arts centers, four of which serve culturally specific communities, have joined forces to share space and resources.

On a walk down the hallway, you're likely to bump into filmmakers on break from their stint in an FAF editing room or overhear languages from all over the world, particularly when the San Francisco International Asian American Film Festival, Festival! Cine Latino!, or Jewish Film Festival are under way. People in the film industry who have visited the cooperative mention how impressed they are by the shared independent spirit it embodies. Many visiting filmmakers and newcomers to the area include a stop at the building on their must-see list.

Independent Feature Project (IFP) and **Independent Feature Film Market (IFFM)**
are for independent feature filmmakers, directors, screen-writers, producers, agents, development executives, distribu-tors, festival programmers, TV and home video buyers, and other film professionals.

104 West 29th Street
12th Floor
New York, NY 10001
Phone: 212-465-8200
Fax: 212-465-8525
Web site: http://www.ifp.org

Contact: Michelle Byrd, Deputy Director
Founded: 1979; Open: Services year-round, but IFFM in September; Deadlines: For market entries, end of May for early submission, mid-June for final submission; Cost: IFP Membership Dues $100; IFFM Market Pass $65–$200; Film or script entry fee $250–$425; Job Placement: No.

As noted in the listing for IFP/West, IFP is a national membership organization with chapters in Los Angeles, Chicago, Minneapolis/St. Paul, and Miami Beach. It was founded on the belief that "a truly vital American cinema must include the personal, idiosyncratic, sometimes contro-versial voices of filmmakers working outside the established system." IFP accordingly supports the voices of these outsiders by promoting them in a marketplace that is at best puzzled by and at worst hostile to unfamiliar kinds of films.

Straddling the line between the business and creative communities, this organization uses its significant international connections to get films financed and picked up for distribution, improving the possibilities of the films taking their places in the marketplace and being seen by audiences. Before independent filmmakers show their new works at film festivals, the IFP's annual Independent Feature Film Market allows them to test their appeal to buyers from around the world by giving buyers a "first look" at just completed and in-progress features and shorts, as well as scripts in the pipeline.

IFFM also provides daily seminars and workshops to introduce filmmakers and screenwriters to top industry professionals and presents insider panels on optioning scripts, negotiating deals, and financing and distributing independent films. The "Meet the Buyers" series, for example, includes representatives from such companies as Fine Line, HBO, Miramax, and Sony Pictures Classics. A daily or full Market Pass grants admission to these sessions, along with market screenings, all held at the Angelika Film Center in New York.

Similarly, IFP offers a variety of monthly industry seminars and workshops, such as the popular "From Script to Screen" conference on screenplay development and screenings of new independent films.

CONVENTIONS AND FILM FESTIVALS

International Documentary Association/Congress (IDA) is for international documentary producers, scholars, writers, critics, and industry professionals.

1551 South Robertson Boulevard
Suite 201
Los Angeles, CA 90035
Phone: 310-284-8422
Fax: 310-785-9334
E-mail: idf@netcom.com
Web site: http://www/documentary.org

Contact: Betsy McLane
Founded: 1982; Open: Conferences are convened every few
years; Deadlines: two to three weeks in advance; Cost:
Packages $225–$350, single-day fees $40–$120; Panels,
private sessions, roundtables, keynote $10–$35.

For documentary producers, the International Documentary
Congress, which meets every few years, provides a chance to
meet and exchange ideas with some of the world's most
accomplished practitioners of the art form. The Los
Angeles-based International Documentary Association, an
organization of about 1,500 members in thirty countries,
convenes the congress.

The congress takes an eye-opening look at the changing
environment in which documentaries are funded, produced,
and seen throughout the world. Documentary makers have
much to be uneasy about, from shrinking public funds to the
pull toward Nielsen-driven sensationalism, and recent sessions have dealt with these issues and others. The congress
offers a rare chance to talk with mentors and peers about
subjects as complex as ethical challenges embedded in making
true films and the frontiers being opened by new technologies.

In keeping with its mission, the congress also shuns the
superficial in its screenings of genre-bending documentaries
and in the speakers it chooses. Recent speakers have included
such luminaries as Marcel Ophuls (*The Sorrow and the Pity*),
newsman Daniel Schorr, and British director Michael Apted
(*28 Up*). If you are interested in documentaries, you should
contact IDA for information about the congress and its
year-round publications, seminars and lectures, and filmmaker services.

ShowBiz Expo West
is held in Los Angeles every spring and ShowBiz Expo East in
New York every fall.

383 Main Avenue
Norwalk, CT 06851
Phone: 800-840-5688, 203-840-5662
Fax: 203-840-9662
E-mail: inquiry@showbiz.reedexpo.com
Web site: http://showbiz.reedexpo.com
Contact: Reed Exhibition Companies
Founded: Circa 1980; Open: N/A; Cost: Varies.

These conventions are designed for professionals engaged in every aspect of entertainment production and at every level of technical expertise and career development. For the price of admission, you can attend workshops and seminars and walk around the convention floor to pick up information and meet new people who can be helpful to your career. With about thirty sessions, these are "must attend" events for any newcomer to the film industry.

The Sundance Institute Feature Film Program
is for feature filmmakers, screenwriters, producers, and artists in transition to film, with administrative headquarters in Santa Monica and offices and programs in Salt Lake City.

225 Santa Monica Boulevard, 8th Floor
Santa Monica, CA 90401
Phone: 310-394-4662
Fax: 310-394-8353
E-mail: sundance@deltanet.com
Web site: http://www.sundance.org

Contact: Michelle Satter, Director
Founded: 1981; Open: January and June sessions; Cost: Admission application $25, with a letter describing the proposed project and the reason for applying to the program, resumes of the writer and other key people attached to the project, project/screenplay synopsis, and the first five pages of the script; Deadlines: June for January session, November for June session; the Sundance Institute

pays for travel, room, and board for one writer/filmmaker for each accepted project, of which there are from twenty to thirty each year.

In 1981, Robert Redford first assembled a group of colleagues and friends in Utah to discuss ideas for revitalizing American film. With their eyes on emerging screenwriters and visionary directors, they laid the framework for the Sundance Institute, and the American independent film movement hasn't been the same since. The institute is best known to the public for its Sundance Film Festival, which first drew serious attention in the industry as a result of its first showing of Steven Soderbergh's later very successful *sex, lies and videotape*.

Each year the Institute's Feature Film Program offers two dozen screenwriters and filmmakers a chance to delve into their craft through the June Filmmakers Lab and the January and June Screenwriters Labs. All three focus on compelling, original, feature-length narrative stories that represent the unique vision of the writer and/or director.

The Filmmakers Lab is a three-week, hands-on workshop for directors and writers, who take scenes from their screenplays and rehearse, shoot, and edit them on videotape, all with the creative input of veteran directors, editors, cinematographers, writers, producers, and an ensemble of professional actors. The Screenwriters Labs, which are five days long, are structured as writers' workshops, with one-on-one problem-solving sessions with seasoned screenwriters. (The last week of the Filmmakers Lab incorporates the June Screenwriters Lab.)

Also included in the Feature Film Program is a three-day Producers Conference in July, in which lab participants and others who sign up join professionals to discuss the marketplace for independent films and strategies for moving their projects into production. The institute does not provide funding but does provide filmmakers with a chance to see, hear, and work with their script "on its feet" and helps them put together the creative and business teams and financing to get their film produced.

Just up the hill, but a million miles from Sundance's headquarters, you'll find The Slamdance Festival. This festival was started in the early 1990s by a small group of independent filmmakers whose works were shunned by Sundance. Protesting against Sundance's disproportionate influence, Slamdance also shows some terrific films in and out of competition. For more information on Slamdance: E-mail: slamdance@earthlink.net; Web site: http://www.slamdance. com.

For filmmakers whose work Slamdance also turns down there is now the Slumdance Festival, which surfaced in 1997 as a new gem among Park City's film festivals. For more information on Slumdance: E-mail: lovemail@slumdance.com or hatemail@slumdance.com; Web site: http://www.slumdance. com.

The SXSW Film Festival and Conference
is for independent film producers and directors, screen-writers, and motion picture professionals.

P.O. Box 4999
Austin, TX 78765
Phone: 512-467-7979
Fax: 512-451-0754
E-mail: 72662.2465@compuserve.com
Web site: http://www.sxsw.com

Contact: Nancy Schafer, Executive Producer
Founded: 1993; Open: March; Cost: $125–$175 for festival and conference admission.

This film festival has sent Austin to the head of the class in the not-New York and not-Los Angeles entertainment world. The purpose of the burgeoning festival is to champion "the self-contained, revolutionary social vision of an independently produced American cinema."

As such, it not only screens independent films but also offers panel discussions, workshops, roundtables, and mentoring sessions with industry professionals and independent movers and shakers. These include everything from workshops on sound editing, working with unions, and budgeting features to lectures by speakers with the lowdown on underground distribution resources.

Attending seminars, conventions, and film festivals is another way of networking, so when you go, be sure to bring plenty of business cards, put on your best face, and wear clothes that are cleaned and pressed. Not only will you will have a great time, you'll also be expanding your network in a way that you can't do every day.

chapter 7

Industry Trade Papers and Online Services

No matter what part of the film business you're trying to break into, you must read the trade papers. If you don't, you'll be at a significant professional disadvantage, because the trades tell you what's going on in the industry. If you don't know what's going on in the industry, there's no way you can ever succeed in the film business. It's as simple as that. Face the fact that you'll have to dish out the money and order both of the trades, *Daily Variety* and the *Hollywood Reporter*. If you can't afford both, and they're expensive, subscribe to at least one of them, because they're the lifelines of the business—the who, what, and where of the film industry.

As in every industry, there are a number of advantages to reading the trade papers. First, as noted above, they enable you to keep up with what's going on in the industry in general. Second, by reading them you'll be able to identify the industry's most important people, the ones who are making the decisions. Third, they provide you with the latest news in your chosen area of the industry. Fourth, because everyone reads them, information published in the trades is frequently referred to, and you'll want to know what people are talking about. Finally, although the best jobs usually don't show up in the "Help Wanted" sections of the trades, those sections, along with the production listings, both of which are discussed below, will provide you with a starting point for seeing what kinds of jobs are available.

While it's not necessary for you to read the trades from cover to cover, you should certainly read the main articles and the important columns (like Robert Osborne's "Rambling Reporter" in the *Hollywood Reporter*) and at least scan everything else. You never know when something you read in the trades will turn out to be useful in building your career, and you never want to pass up an opportunity to do that.

THE HELP WANTED SECTION

As in every industry, the best jobs in film are rarely listed in the "Help Wanted" sections of the trades—you're much more likely to find those openings through networking. However, looking through these sections is still the quickest way to start searching for a way to break into the business. If you see an ad that you find interesting, there's certainly no reason why you shouldn't respond to it. After all, what do you have to lose?

If you're just starting out, stick with the job listings that offer internships or entry-level jobs. Getting hired as an intern or at an entry-level position is a way to get your foot in the door. You can always move up from there. Unfortunately, most entry-level positions are for people who are willing to make coffee, file, or answer phones, but that's how you get started. It's called "paying your dues," and everyone has done it.

Here are a couple of typical ads:

**NEW POLICE ACTION SERIES
SEEKING INTERNS**

Office experience preferred.

Mail resume to:

STRIKE FORCE
Associated Television International
2233 Sunset Blvd., 14th Floor
Hollywood, CA 90028

INTERN NEEDED

For Gen-X film co. specializing in extreme sports, documentaries, commercials. P/T or F/T. No pay, must have own vehicle. Grt. opportunity.

Fax Michelle at 310-555-2233

Of course, whenever you do respond to an ad, your response should be as professional as you can make it, whether it's on the phone, through e-mail or ground mail, or in person. You should always do whatever it is the ad tells you to do about making contact. If the ad says either mail or fax your resume, then do it. And if an ad says, "No Walk-ins," don't go to the office to sell yourself. If you go to the office when the production company has specifically asked you not to, you'll be shooting yourself in the foot—you won't get the job.

As you look through the trades, in addition to the "Help Wanted" ads you will probably see some "Position Wanted" ads. Placing such an ad might seem like a good idea, but it really isn't. Not only are these ads expensive, they make you look desperate, which is not the way to position yourself in Hollywood. In due time you will run an ad, but it will be for a "congratulations" or a "thank you."

THE PRODUCTION LISTINGS

After you've looked over the "Help Wanted" ads, you'll want to look at the production listings. Both *Daily Variety* and the *Hollywood Reporter* have weekly listings of the television shows and movies that are currently in production, so when you're looking for a position and see information about a production that you're interested in, you can contact the production companies directly.

Television Production Listings

These production listings are not the same as "Help Wanted" ads, but they are one way to find jobs in the industry. In the case of television production listings, the network or production location and phone number are listed first, followed by the productions for which they are responsible, which are listed alphabetically. If the listing is new, it's boxed, and if it's been changed since the previous week, it has an asterisk. Here's a sample television production listing:

TotalWorks Television
200 Universal City Plaza, Bldg. 477
Universal City, CA 91608
818-555-5000

So you know . . . (ABC) Series
Ex.prd., Peter Harbert; Prd., Suzy Jones; Coprd., Tom Hayman; Cstg., Marc Alsworth

TotalWorks Television has only one listing here, so if you're interested in working on the television show *So you know . . .* , call the production office and ask to speak to the assistant to the producer (Prd.).

Here is a more extensive TV production listing:

Fran Clark Prods.
2002 W. Olive Ave. Burbank, CA 91510
818-555-3003, Fax: 555-8609

Beyond (FOX) Series

ExPrd., Fran Clark; Supv. Prd., Al Adelman; Cstg., Eddie James; ExCharg. Prd., Zoe Thomas

*Lab Libs (Disney) Series

ExPrd., Fran Clark; ExCharg. Prd., Don Shepard

Hostess from Hell (ABC) Special

ExPrd., Fran Clark, Steve Wilson; Prd., Tom Ruppert; ExCharg. Prd., Zoe Thomas

---

As you can see from the above, Fran Clark Productions has two shows that have already been listed, one of which has been changed, and one new show (the ABC special). If you're interested in finding work on one of these productions, you might call to speak to the assistant to the producer of *Hostess from Hell* and ask if there are any openings for interns or entry-level positions. While you're at it, you can also ask about the *Lab Libs* (Disney) Series and *Beyond* (FOX).

Film Production Listings

Film production listings are similar to television listings, but they generally contain considerably more information about the film. Here are a couple of typical movie production listings:

Monumental Pictures
100002 W. Washington Blvd., Culver City, CA 90232
310-555-4000

Elmo in Weirdland (Family)
Monumental Pictures
Shooting in Wilmington, N.C.
(Start: June 1, 1998)

ExPrd., Bob Jones, Stephanie Smith, Martin Jones; Prd., Mel Kalins, Alex Rock; CoPrd., Tom Clash; Dir., Gary Anson; Scr., Mitchell Joseph; U.S. Dstrb., Starlight Pictures

Max 2000 Pictures
P.O. Box 160, Beverly Hills, CA 90213-0900
310-555-1000

*Anytown, USA (Drama)

Max 2000 Pictures
Shooting in Los Angeles
(Start: June 29, 1998)

ExPrd., Ginny Master; Prd., Laurence Reilly; AsPrd., Petra Thomas; Dir., Wayne Jeffries; Scr., Alvin Deakins; Ed., Nick Bloom; AD., Betsy Burt; U.S. Dstrb., Max 2000 Pictures.

As with the television production listings, if you're interested in working on one of these films you can call the phone number listed and ask for the production office for the movie. Then you can speak to the assistant to the producer or to someone else if you're interested in a specific area of the film.

The trades list so many television and film productions that you should have any number of people to contact about jobs. While you search, make mental notes of the names of the producer, director, cinematographer, etc. If you notice a familiar name, use that to your advantage by stating over the phone that you notice that so-and-so is doing such-and-such on the production, and that you'd love to work with him or her because you liked the work they did on such-and-such a film.

Web Sites

In addition to the "Help Wanted" and Production Listings carried in the two trade publications, both also have Web sites. Web sites have the advantage of being updated more regularly, so if you subscribe to them you can get more up-to-date information than you'll find in the newsstand publications.

Variety's Web site is called *VarietyExtra*, and can be reached at www.variety.com. The subscription tier of the Web site gives you full access to the listings at any time, but *Variety* also offers a "Day Pass Ticket" to *VarietyExtra*, which allows for a 24-hour period of access at a cost of only $6. For more information, see the Day Pass Ticket on the first page of *Variety*'s Web site or call 800-552-3632.

The Hollywood Reporter has *The Hollywood Reporter* Web site, which can be reached at www.hollywoodreporter.com. Like *VarietyExtra*, a subscription gives you full access to the listings at any time, but *The Hollywood Reporter* does not offer day passes. You can, however, get full information on how to subscribe at the Web site. The Web site also sends out free e-mail bulletins from Monday through Friday, which provide major breaking news stories.

OTHER PUBLICATIONS TO READ

There are several other trade publications which, while not essential reading, also have value as sources of information. These include *Weekly Variety* (which covers the whole industry), *Film & Video* (production), *Filmmaker* (the independent scene), *Film Comment* (general), *Cinefex* (special effects), and *Cinefantastique* (fantasy, science fiction, and horror films and television).

Industry insiders also generally read *Premiere* magazine and *Entertainment Weekly*, primarily for their "Calendar" sections, as well as *The Los Angeles Times*' business section and the magazine, book, and arts sections of the Sunday edition of *The New York Times*.

You might also want to consider reading the newsletters published by the various guilds, unions, and associations in the entertainment industry so you'll know about current and upcoming events that may be of interest to you. These can be ordered directly from the organizations, but industry libraries also carry these important publications.

DATABASES AND ONLINE SERVICES

In addition to publications, there are several other sources of information on the film industry that can be accessed by computer or telephone, including several databases. Note that there is often a fee or subscription price for these services.

- *BASELINE* is the best known of these. It calls itself "the largest central source of information ever developed for the entertainment industry and the only on-line service designed specifically to meet the needs of film and television professionals."

BASELINE's research and information service can provide answers to your questions in print, over the phone, or on line at www.pkbaseline.com/baseline.html. It has information on people and their credits (including how to reach them), products (who made what features, pilots, and TV specials and series, as well as who is working on what right now), numbers (box office, demographics, and show business stock prices), news, release schedules, screening dates, and e-mail. When you're job hunting you'll also want to find out more about BASELINE's Inpro database, which lists projects according to their status (e.g., in development, preproduction, production, postproduction, or on hold).

Here's an abbreviated sample listing of an actual movie that's been completed:

Drunks
COUNTRY OF ORIGIN: United States
STATUS: wrapped
U.S. RELEASE DATE: January 1997 (winter/theatrical)
U.S. DISTRIBUTOR: Northern Arts Entertainment (USA)
VIDEO DISTRIBUTOR: BMG Entertainment (video-USA)
PRODUCTION COMPANIES:
> Sea Goat Films
> Kardana Productions
> The Shooting Gallery

PRODUCERS:
> Shireen Meistrich—producer
> Burtt Harris—producer
> Peter Cohn—producer
> Larry Meistrich—executive producer
> Tom Carouso—executive producer
> John N. Hart Jr.—executive producer
> Ilene Landress—co-producer
> Gary Lennon—co-producer

DIRECTOR: Peter Cohn
CAST INFORMATION:
> Richard Lewis—Jim
> Faye Dunaway—Becky
> Calista Flockhart—Helen
> Spalding Gray—Louis
> George Martin—Marty
> Amanda Plummer—Shelley
> Parker Posey—Debbie
> Howard Rollins—Joseph
> Anna Thomson—Tanya
> Dianne Wiest—Rachel
> Sam Rockwell—Tony

In addition to its online database, BASELINE publishes books for those in the business, including *Who's Who in American Film Now: All the People Who Make Movies*, which lists more than 11,000 creative and technical people.

- *Celebrity Service International* (CSI), which was established in 1937, has another online database that provides up-to-date biographies, contact people, and current where-abouts of celebrities and major Hollywood players. However, access to the database is by subscription only, and CSI won't accept you as a subscriber unless you can convince them that you're already an established entertainment-industry figure with a known firm or project. The contact is Jeff Kormos, CSI, 8833 Sunset Boulevard, Suite 401, Los Angeles, California 90069, 310-652-1700.

You can also find other online services by doing a search on the Internet. The Internet is constantly changing, which means you never know what new entertainment industry services might appear.

THE ULTIMATE SOURCE OF JOB LEADS

Unquestionably, the best source for information about openings in the film industry is the United Talent Agency (UTA) list. It's published as a printout every month or so and lists virtually every job worth trying for in the business at any given moment. The UTA list has been around about ten years and is where the major companies and productions place their "Help Wanted" ads.

The major problem is that the list is almost impossible to get unless you're one of UTA's clients or are already connected to the major players. Hollywood is a real "insider" town, and the UTA list is a prime example of Hollywood's version of Catch-22. To make it, you need to know somebody. And how do you get to know somebody? By knowing somebody. It can make you crazy.

Even without access to the UTA list, there are many sources of information on the industry in general and on job openings on specific productions. If you plan to make your career in the film industry, it is essential that you not only familiarize yourself with all of them but that you make every effort to keep up to date with the information they provide. In the film industry, knowledge *is* power, and if someone else has knowledge that you don't, it can mean the difference between a successful career and one that never gets off the ground.

chapter 8

Lights, Camera, Action!

You may already be familiar with a variation of the old paradox about the difficulties of breaking into the film industry: No experience? You can't get an interview. No interview? You can't get a job. No job? You can't get the experience. But you need experience to get a job. It can go on and on, around and around. Nevertheless, people do break into the film business, and you can, too.

Sometimes people get lucky and just fall into jobs in the film industry (there are a few such stories below), but it doesn't happen very often. As a rule, if you want it to happen, you're going to have to make it happen. As we've already mentioned, one way of getting started is to arrange for an internship with a production company or other organization, an unpaid position that will help you build your resume, gain experience, and develop important new contacts. Internships, however, can be extremely hard to find and nearly impossible to land because of the intense competition in the field.

THE INSTANT APPRENTICESHIP

What's a career-launcher to do? One innovative option is to propose your own internship. This is a technique that has worked for a number of aspiring behind-the-scenes movie workers, because film production companies are often amenable to accepting free help during peak "rush" periods. The contacts you develop during such "unofficial" internships can be extremely valuable in building your career.

As in everything, there are several ways to go about arranging your own internship. Sometimes people simply approach film crews while they're shooting and offer to help. While an offer can be refused, if you're persistent the chances are that eventually they'll give in and let you do some work around the shoot. It may not be exactly the kind of work you had in mind, but once you get on a set with a production company you have the opportunity to meet people who are working in the industry. Contacts, as we've said before, lead to other contacts, and eventually to the job you really want.

You may not, however, want to start out quite that aggressively, so here's another approach. Because it's not as aggressive, it might not be as effective, but it's still worth a try. Some people have done it, and it's worked. Check the "Help Wanted" ads in the trades for senior or mid-level openings (not internships) in your field of interest. Why? Because, chances are if they're recruiting for someone, they're short-handed and could use help in that department.

When you spot such an ad, call the office manager or other hiring authority directly. Once you get him or her on the phone, say that you're interested in being an intern, but also say that you understand how busy they are and that you'd be happy to meet with an assistant to discuss it further. Ask whom you should speak to about this option and tell them that you'll follow up yourself. Don't forget to do it! Despite all its members, the film industry is a close-knit community, and it's important that when you develop a reputation, it's as a professional, not as a flake.

Even if you don't see a particular "Help Wanted" ad that you're interested in, you can call the Human Resources Department of a production company and offer yourself as an intern in your field of interest. For example, if researching information for television shows interests you, you might call E! Entertainment Television and offer to be an intern in its research department.

Whichever tactic you choose, make sure you keep at it. With the right attitude, odds are you will eventually run into someone who will take you up on your offer. Once you get an internship, get to know as many people as you can. Remember that in the film industry it's all about networking, and the more people you get to know the more likely you'll find work in your chosen field. Here are some stories of people who did it because they asked, searched, persisted, and finally landed a job on the set.

STROKE OF THE BRUSH

Steve studied art in high school, worked as a construction draftsman and illustrator in the army, and spent a year at the Art Institute in Chicago before settling down in Seattle. Although he had not been intent on getting a job in the film industry, one day a carpenter he knew mentioned that he was about to start working on a local television show called *Glory Days*, and Steve told him that if they needed painters he should have them give him a call. Somewhat to his surprise, they did call, and he went to work as a set painter.

Steve really enjoyed working on the show, and one day while he was talking to the production designer he mentioned that he would really like to work with him again. Sometime later, when the production designer got a job in Portland on a show called *Permanent Records*, he called Steve in, but this time as the head painter. One thing led to another, and he subsequently worked on *The Hand That Rocks the Cradle* (1992), which established him as the lead painter in the Northwest and got him work on *The Temp* (1993).

While working on *The Temp*, he was contacted by the designer for *Sleepless in Seattle* (1993), who had gotten his name from the designer for *Hand*. Not surprisingly, Steve stresses that word of mouth has a great deal of impact on whether or not you work in the industry. It's certainly worked for him. In addition to working in Seattle and Portland, Steve has done features in Minneapolis, Memphis, Cincinnati, Salt Lake City, and Hong Kong and has since settled in Los Angeles.

When asked to explain his success, Steve says that he always remembers that films are a team project and that if you get a reputation for being hard to work with or self-centered, the word gets around. "It's also," he says, "important to learn to deal with high pressure, short time frames, and last-minute changes."

MONSTER MAKER

Theresa was living in Los Angeles and working at a cosmetics counter when she got involved in doing makeup for school plays.

While making up the performers she learned about the different kinds of stage makeup and how to apply them and in the process discovered how much she liked doing it.

Deciding that she wanted to make this her career in films, Theresa got in touch with some of the major studios. However, they wouldn't hire her because she wasn't a union member, and she needed to have a job to be in the union. Instead, she contacted several independent movie companies, because those who work on films for independents don't have to be union members. With some persistence, she managed to talk her way into a job as a makeup assistant on a biker movie, helping the makeup artist do whatever needed to be done.

As these things happen, one thing led to another, and eventually she got a job working on a horror film, helping to create and do the makeup for the monster. Although the work wasn't easy, she really enjoyed herself. Today she's still working for independent movie companies on horror, science fiction, and biking films. She still doesn't have a union card, but she's making a good living doing what she does best—creating monsters.

Theresa's advice for those who want to do special effects makeup is to get a job selling cosmetics. "Once you've learned the basics," she says, "you can offer to do makeup for school and community theaters, or talk your friends into letting you practice on them. The important thing," she asserts, "is to practice your craft."

SPOTTING THE RIGHT LOCATION

Sometimes people just luck into jobs in the film industry. Kathy was out taking pictures of homes for her business when a studio scout asked her if she would like to take pictures of possible locations for a major studio film that was coming to town. Because her current occupation paid well, she asked how much they were willing to pay her. When she found out that she'd be paid by the hour rather than by the shot, she jumped at the chance and has been a location scout and manager since.

Because she's not in a major city, Kathy works with the local film commission office to encourage production companies to come to her city. The office relies on her to do most of the footwork because it doesn't have the funds to pay a full-time employee. She will often spend an afternoon taking pictures, laser copying them, and sending them to production companies in Los Angeles. Unfortunately, even after all that hustling around, the production companies sometimes decide against using the area, so Kathy has to hustle some more.

When she is working on a film, Kathy will spend anywhere from two weeks to three months on it. Wherever she goes she takes her camera, and on occasion she's been asked to become the production photographer on the spot, which makes her paycheck even bigger.

Because she's now considered an "insider," everyone in town who wants to work on films being shot there has Kathy's number in their Rolodex. She says that sometimes she feels guilty because she can't always refer work to everyone, but she does have a select few whom she calls her "best referrals."

GOTTA WEAR CLOTHES

Claudia became a costume designer by chance. She always enjoyed sewing, made costumes for her high school productions, and worked during summer vacations altering costumes for the local theater-in-the-park. When she realized that she was happy whenever she was involved in designing costumes, she decided that she wanted to make a career in films as a costume designer.

Unfortunately, because she lived in the Midwest, far from any production companies, she realized that she'd have to move, so when she graduated from high school she went to live in New York City. She was lucky and got a job as a wardrobe production assistant, also known as a "PA," running errands, shopping for supplies for actors' and actresses' wardrobes, and buying clothes as needed. Sometimes it was hard to find the kind of clothes the production needed, but she never gave up and never returned empty-handed.

Although it gave her an opportunity to learn her craft, being a PA was difficult at first because she wasn't earning much money and had to find temp work to make enough to support herself. Eventually, she made enough personal contacts to get steady work. Moving from film to film—and without any formal training except for two semesters of sewing class in high school—she slowly but surely made her way up to wardrobe assistant, wardrobe supervisor, assistant costume designer, and, finally, costume designer.

Her first job as a costume designer was on a low-budget independent feature film. Because the budget was so low, she did everything that had to be done with the costumes herself, putting together more than fifty costumes in just four weeks. She was lucky because since the film was set in the present day, she was able to use many of the actors' personal wardrobes.

Claudia's job as a costume designer is both creative and managerial, and she makes good money now because she's in the union. As a rule, she works between two to four months and then has a month off. As you'd expect, she loves it. It took hard work, but she got there.

PROPS ARE IMPORTANT, TOO

Kevin always had an interest in antiques and liked to work with clay and papier-mâché. When he received an associate degree in interior design, he was able to find a job with an interior design company. While on the job, among many other things, he made clay sculptures for the company's window display.

One day a production assistant in the props department of a local film company noticed one of his clay vases in the window, came in and asked about it, and commissioned him to make one for a film. Although it had not occurred to him before that, Kevin realized that supplying props for films could be quite profitable.

Kevin began reading *Variety* and other industry trades and searched out the productions he read about. He also called local unions, the Directors Guild, production companies, and local commercial houses for television commercials, asking all of them to put his name on their help-available lists.

He says he got his first jobs by networking, making it his business to meet people who knew about jobs. When he started out as a props person he earned between $75 and $100 for a 10- to 14-hour day. Over time he built up his resume by buying and making props for nonunion films and videos. He made faces for costumes and masks, and, on one occasion, chickens for a television commercial.

Although he wanted to join a union, he wasn't able to because he hadn't had a real job in the industry. Eventually, though, he was able to get a job as a production assistant in the props department on a local film, at which point the union let him work as a "permittee," a status under which he had to pay the union a small percentage of his paycheck. He wasn't, however, allowed to join the union until he finished his first film.

Now he pays the union about $500 a year in dues, which in turn provides him with medical benefits and legal representation (even between contracts) and job leads when production companies are looking for a props person. He also gets overtime pay after 10 hours, regular breaks, and good meals and is making three times as much per day as he did when he started out. Eventually, Kevin is hoping to become an art director, but in the meantime he's making a steady living and enjoying what he's doing.

FROM CHICAGO TO HOLLYWOOD

Mike came to Hollywood from Chicago without any definite plans but with a strong desire to work in the film industry. After working at a series of temporary jobs in the business, mostly wandering around in search of what he wanted to do, he finally landed a job as a production assistant. Although he was still unsure of what he really wanted to do, he worked hard, did a good job, and as a result was offered a job as a camera assistant.

On his new job, Mike was responsible for keeping track of camera shots and in the process learned how to set up the "road map" for editors and other postproduction people. Eventually, this experience led him to become an ADR/Foley sound recordist, which he now does on a permanent basis.

When Mike started working as an ADR/Foley sound recordist, his company was nonunion, but the local sound union eventually stepped in to organize the company, and Mike was able to join. While this opened many opportunities for other types of jobs, Mike's first love is ADR/Foley, and he's really not interested in doing anything else. Although he admits the hours are very long—sometimes he works 15-hour days—now that he's a union member he is compensated by being paid overtime. Even more important, he's working in the film industry, which is what he always wanted to do.

WHAT ABOUT THE LOOK?

As a boy, Ted was never particularly interested in the movies—he was much more interested in soccer and the Boy Scouts. After high school, though, he got a job in the shipping department at Technicolor, packing and logging shipments. From there, he went on to a job in the shipping department at Movie Lab.

After working at Movie Lab for a while, he heard about an opening for an entry-level position as an optical timer's assistant, and since it paid more than he was making in the shipping department, he decided to give it a try. It wasn't a terribly exciting job—his main function was to go to film screenings and takes notes about what people said regarding what had to be done to the films—but he'd been bitten by the bug and began actively pursuing a career in the industry.

Moving from one job to another, learning as much as he could at each job, and making as many contacts as he could, he moved up through the ranks until he got involved in doing optical effects timing. "It's not the kind of thing you learn from a book," Ted says. "Like most jobs in the movies, you just learn how to do the job by doing it." And he's enjoying every minute of it.

WITH A LITTLE HELP FROM HIS FRIENDS

Tom had always wanted to produce his own movies, so when a friend told him about a job at Warner Bros. working on the *Lois and Clark* TV series as an assistant to the executive producers, he jumped at it.

Once he got into the studio, he made it his business to learn everything he could about filmmaking and to get to know as many people as he could. When he found a script he liked for a film called *Border to Border*, about two guys bicycling from Canada to Mexico, he moved into action.

Getting a friend to lend him a professional camera and talking Warner Bros. into letting him use an editing suite for free, he got his longtime friend and high school chum, Karen, whom he had helped get a job as a production assistant on *Lois and Clark*, to become the producer and the all-around do-it-if-no-one-else-is-available person.

Next, he enlisted almost everyone else he knew at the company to help him make the film. Of course, not everyone was willing to do it, but when he was turned down he just asked someone else, and kept asking until he found someone willing to help. Several months and $250,000 later, he had his feature film, *Border to Border*, which is even now being shown at film festivals. Not surprisingly, the one bit of advice that Tom has to share is, "Never give up."

Everyone who breaks into the film industry has his or her own story. Even though many of them are similar, no two are exactly alike. There is one thread that runs through all of these stories: If you want to be in the movie industry and you're willing to work hard, learn from everyone and everything around you, make as many contacts as you can, and generally pay your dues, you can do it. You can make your dream a reality.

chapter 9

The Interview and Beyond

You've finally got that interview for a position as a production assistant on a major motion picture! This is the interview that has kept you staring at the telephone, waiting and praying night and day for it to ring. Now it's time to land that job, the job that will lead you to other jobs. Your moment of truth has arrived. So it's important that you make the most of this interview.

Success in the film industry is 80 percent preparation and 20 percent show, so it's essential that you go into the interview completely prepared. Be ready. Know what's expected of you before you go. Why? Because if you want to be successful, you'll have to control the process as much as possible, and the only way to do that is to have knowledge—and knowledge is control.

Now take a deep breath, relax, and think about this: You can always walk away from the job if you decide you're not interested. What? Walk away from a job? You have to remember that you always have that choice, because if you go into an interview thinking "I must have this job," it will work against you. Of course, this doesn't mean that you shouldn't do your best in the interview. You should always do that. But the image you want to project is one of confidence and self-assurance, and if you come across as being desperate you'll have given up any measure of control that you may have had.

Think of the interview as a major performance at the Hollywood Bowl. You've studied, you've rehearsed, you know your audience, and the curtain is about to go up.

THE KEY TO SUCCESSFUL INTERVIEWING

Odd as it may sound, successful interviewing has nothing to do with your experience, your knowledge of films, your talent, the film classes you took, or any of the other basic necessities. You needed all those things to get the interview, but you need something else to get the job. And that something else can be summed up in one word: attitude. There's an enormous amount of competition for jobs in the film industry, and there are always going to be people out there who have more experience, more knowledge, and maybe even more talent, so what you have to do is work on developing a highly positive attitude.

Since there are plenty of other people with the ability to do almost any job—especially at the entry level—employers differentiate between candidates by their attitudes toward the job. Names, faces, and resumes can all become a blur to a production manager who's interviewed ten, twenty, or even 100 candidates, but a positive attitude stays in the manager's mind. If you come across as having an attitude of wanting to do your very best for the company, of being focused on doing whatever it takes to get the job done, and of being able to handle yourself and any situation that may come up, you'll be the one chosen.

Why is attitude so important? Because most film production companies or studios already have more than their fair share of multitalented superstars who care about no one but themselves. Ask any production manager who the most valuable member of his team is, and he won't point to the overrated superstar but to the person with the "can do" attitude, the person who can be counted on in any situation, the person who truly strives for excellence. A team player who's working at 99 percent efficiency will be regarded much more highly any day of the week than a flashy superstar who's working at 50 percent of capacity any day of the week.

You can show your winning attitude in the way you present yourself. Use positive language and talk about excellence and trying to do your best. Show by your stories and examples how you've put those words into practice. Let the interviewer know when, where, and how you've put forth that extra effort. If you can show the interviewer, by words and examples, your "can do" attitude, you'll be hired, while all of the superstars will receive polite rejection letters to add to their growing collections.

BEFORE YOUR FIRST INTERVIEW

In preparing for an interview, the first thing you should do is try to anticipate the questions the interviewer will ask. You've probably been on some interviews before, for summer or part-time jobs, for example, so you should have some idea of the kinds of questions that are likely to come up. If you've done your homework, you'll also have a fairly good idea of what the job entails, so you'll also know what the interviewer will be looking for. Don't just think about the questions—write them down so you'll be able to refer to them later.

Practice, Practice

The next step is to go through a rehearsal interview. Ask a friend, family member, or neighbor to play the role of the interviewer. This will give you an opportunity to work on your interviewing skills and answers with a real person who can critique you honestly. It's a lot easier to listen to constructive criticism from someone who you know cares about you and your success. Doing so will also give you a definite advantage over your competition, because very few newcomers to the film industry practice their interviewing skills. The majority of candidates end up stumbling through several interviews before they have any real sense of how they're doing and then learn only because the rejection letters start arriving.

You'll be surprised at how much improvement you'll see even after just one rehearsal interview. Why? As the saying goes, "Practice makes perfect." Think of yourself as an actor or actress preparing for an audition. Just like them, you have to learn your lines and then rehearse and rehearse until you have it down cold. Then, and only then, are you ready to go into the interview.

If you have access to a video camera, it's also a great idea to tape your rehearsal interviews. That way, you will have two opinions—the rehearsal interviewer's and your own. When you see yourself on videotape you may find that you come across very differently than you think you do. It may be better, and it may be worse, but wouldn't you rather know before going into a real interview? If you recognize problems on the tape or things that you can work on, you have the opportunity to do something about them.

It's essential to go through at least one rehearsal interview, but more than one is better. After you've reviewed yourself on tape, take one thing that needs work, correct it, and then go through a second rehearsal interview. If you find something else that needs work, correct it, and then rehearse again. Keep at it until you feel confident that you'll be able to handle whatever may come up in the real interview.

Know Before You Go

There are two types of information you'll want to get before you go to an interview. The first is about the production company or studio and the second is about the person who will be interviewing you.

If you're reading the trades, you should have a pretty good idea of what any given production is about and what any given studio is involved in at the moment. If you don't know, make it your business to find out. Interviewers are impressed when job applicants exhibit knowledge of the company because it means the applicant is serious and willing to put in the effort required to learn. If you can, talk to someone who is already on the inside. If it's a production company that has come to your town to shoot location shots, ask the film commission office or the location scout and manager about anything in particular you should know.

If the interview is at a studio, there are two ways of getting this kind of information. The first is to use your network. If the interview was the result of a network contact, call the contact to thank him for helping you set up the interview and then ask for whatever he can tell you about the interviewer or the studio. If you know someone who works at the studio, ask her.

If and when you do find someone who can provide you with information, call as far in advance of the interview as possible. Make sure you've done your homework so your contact doesn't have to give you the basic information that you should already have. At this point you'll want to ask for specifics about the company and the individual who'll be interviewing you. You might, for example, ask if there's anything particular about the company's culture that you should know. You should ask what kind of person the interviewer is, what he likes or dislikes, and if he has any hot buttons (either good or bad). Remember, the more information you have, the better prepared you'll be. The better prepared you are, the more likely you'll get the job.

Dress for Success

A college campus may be the perfect place for you to showcase your flair for the latest in fashion, but a production manager's office is not, so sandals and sweatshirts are out. While business suits are still appropriate for corporate jobs, when you're interviewing for a film production or at a studio you have to dress the part. A man should wear khakis and a polo shirt or shirt and tie. Shoes should be conservative, clean, and hole-free. A woman should wear a skirt or khaki pants, a cotton blouse, and flats. You don't have to be overly conservative, but you shouldn't be overly casual either. You should be doing the talking, not your clothes.

This is not to say that you need to go out and buy a whole new wardrobe. If you need new clothes, go for quality rather than quantity. Two or three well-chosen interview outfits should be sufficient until you actually get a job. You could probably get away with only one, as long as you make sure to keep it cleaned and pressed. It's a good idea, however, to have a second, because if you are called back for a second interview by the same person you won't want to wear the same outfit.

If you're still not sure about how to dress for the interview, call and ask! Don't call the interviewer, but call the Human Resources Department and say: "I have an interview with _____ in the _____ department for a position as a _____. Could you please tell me what would be appropriate dress for this interview?" You run the risk of someone in Human Resources thinking you're a social imbecile, but that's a lot better than distracting the interviewer with clothes that are inappropriate.

THE INTERVIEW

Now that you've practiced your interviewing skills, learned all you could about the company and the interviewer, and made sure that you're dressed appropriately, you're ready to go out and get that job. There are, however, a few more things you should keep in mind during the interview itself.

Body Language Matters

Communication is what interviews are all about, but communication is more than just what you say. Nonverbal communication, which you are least aware of, can speak the loudest, and there are some things that you should and shouldn't do. (This, incidentally, is when videotaping a mock interview can be particularly helpful, as it will enable you to determine what your body language is saying and show you if any improvements are necessary.)

What You Should Do

There are five types of positive nonverbal communications that are important when it comes to interviewing. Here they are in order of importance.

- **Eye Contact**—The importance of good eye contact cannot be stressed enough. If you look away while listening, it indicates lack of interest and a short attention span. If you fail to maintain eye contact while speaking, it suggests a lack of confidence in what you're saying, or—worse—that you may be lying. Do not assume you have good eye contact. Ask, watch, then practice. Some people maintain excellent eye contact while listening but lose eye contact when speaking, or vice versa. Sit down with a friend and practice until you are comfortable maintaining sincere and attentive eye contact. But avoid staring!

- **Facial Expressions**—Watch out for expressions that are sullen, confused, or even mildly hysterical during your rehearsal interview. Take a good, hard look at yourself in the mirror and try to see yourself as others do. Then, as appropriate, modify your facial expressions. If there are any negative overall characteristics, eliminate them. Always add the one simple expression that nearly every interviewee forgets—a smile! Not some stupid Jim Carrey grin, but a real smile that tells the production manager you're a genuinely happy person who's delighted to be interviewing with him. You don't need to keep the smile plastered on your face during the entire interview, but you should remember to keep coming back to it.

- **Posture**—Your posture sends out signals about how confident you are. Stand tall, walk tall, and most of all, sit tall. Height is not what's important, posture is. When standing, stand up straight. When you're seated, make sure you sit at the front edge of the chair and lean forward slightly.

- **Gestures**—Contrary to popular belief, gestures should be very limited during the interview. Don't use artificial gestures to try to heighten the importance of what you're saying—they will come off as fake. When you use gestures, make sure they're natural and meaningful.

- **Space**—Recognize the boundaries of your personal space and that of others. Be prepared, however, not to back up or move away from someone who has a personal space that's smaller than yours. Hang in there, take a deep breath, and stand your ground. If you have a smaller than average personal space, make sure you keep your distance so that you don't intimidate someone who needs more space to be comfortable.

What You Shouldn't Do

There are three signals that you particularly do not want sent to an interviewer—nervousness, untrustworthiness, and defensiveness. Unfortunately, it's very easy to send these without even being aware of them. If you have the opportunity to videotape your rehearsal interview, keep an eye out for the following in addition to the nonverbal signals mentioned above.

- **Nervousness**—While you're in all likelihood going to be nervous during the interview, it's important that you not appear to be. Because they are indications of nervousness, you should avoid all of the following: smoking, whistling, pinching your skin, fidgeting, jiggling pocket contents, running your tongue along the front of your teeth, clearing your throat, running your fingers through your hair, jingling your bracelets, wringing your hands, biting on pens or other objects, twiddling your thumbs, biting your fingernails, and clicking your tongue.

- **Untrustworthiness and Defensiveness**—It's natural to feel somewhat defensive in an interview situation but, again, you don't want the interviewer to be aware of it. The following are all considered to be indications of untrustworthiness and defensiveness, so you'll want to avoid them: frowning, squinting, grinning in a tight-lipped fashion, crossed your arms in front of your chest, pulling away, keeping your chin down, touching your face, darting your eyes, looking down when speaking, clenching your hands, gesturing with your fist, pointing with your fingers, chopping one hand into the open palm of the other, and rubbing the back of your neck.

Bear in mind, too, that body language goes in both directions. As you talk with an interviewer, be aware of his or her body language and nonverbal hints. Don't try to read more into them than is actually being communicated, but try to develop a sense of the interviewer's reception of you. It's obvious, but one way you can do this is by seeing how he or she reacts when you smile. If he or she smiles back, it's a good sign. If not, it isn't. You should, in any case, do your best to stay connected with your interviewer—both verbally and nonverbally.

Believe in Yourself

Remember that before you can convince an interviewer that you're right for the job, you have to believe it yourself. If you don't believe it, maybe you should be thinking about doing something else for a living. If you do, you have to make sure to communicate it. Those applicants who are reluctant to express confidence in their abilities are, generally speaking, the ones who get the rejection letters. While it's important that you don't appear to be overly confident, no one is going to sell you if you don't sell yourself. Once you've sold the interviewer on you, he or she will sell you on the position and the company, but not until then. So don't expect the interviewer to tell you why you're right for the job. That's what you should do.

Don't Forget to Ask This Question

The opportunity for you to ask questions often comes only at the end of the interview. In fact, you're typically offered the chance when the interview is over: "Is there anything else you'd like to know?" However, there is one question you should ask of every interviewer as early as possible during the interview: "Can you tell me about the position and the type of person you're looking for?"

The reason it's important for you to ask this question is that it can provide you with your single greatest opportunity to understand more about the job and your ability to fill it. By asking the question, you'll learn exactly what the interviewer's specific criteria are, and you'll be able to address them over the course of the interview.

If an obvious opportunity to ask the question doesn't present itself, you should make the opportunity. For example, when you're asked a question like "Have you had any prior experience in the film industry?" you can answer the question, then say, "Can you tell me more about the position and the type of person you're looking for?"

Based on the answer you get, you can frame your answers to further questions around what the interviewer has said he or she wants. For example, if the interviewer tells you that he's looking for someone who is knowledgeable about recent films, you can tell him that you go to the movies very often and rent videos on a regular basis, and mention some of the recent films you've seen (assuming, of course, that it's the truth). The more you're able to demonstrate that you have the qualities, interests, and abilities that an interviewer is looking for, the more likely you are to get the job.

Money Talks

In the film business, if you're being interviewed for a union job, both you and the interviewer know what your wages will be, so the subject never even comes up. The closest you'll get to the discussion of money in an interview is when the interviewer tells you whether or not it is a union job or union set.

If the job is nonunion or you'll be working on a nonunion set, a fair question for you to ask is "What would a person with my background and qualifications typically earn in this position?" Often, the interviewer will be direct about salary and say something like "We're paying $75 a day." Negotiating pay in a nonunion situation is literally impossible. They're doing you a favor by hiring you, so you should be grateful.

A Last Note

As mentioned earlier in reference to networking interviews, it's equally if not more important that you send a thank-you note after a job interview. As with networking interviews, you should send the note as soon as possible after the interview. Surprisingly, many people neglect to do this, even though you'd think it would just be common courtesy. This can, however, actually work to your advantage.

Let's say, for example, that of all the people a production manager interviewed he was most impressed with you and one other person. Perhaps the other person doesn't bother to send a thank-you note, but you do. If you were that production manager, which of the two most likely candidates would you hire? The answer should be obvious.

All things being equal, sending a thank-you note won't get you a job, but it may be the one thing that will tip the balance in your favor. Remember that the film industry is an extremely competitive business, and you can use all the help you can get.

AFTER THE INTERVIEW

There are two possible outcomes to any interview—either you get the job or you don't. If you get the job, it's time for celebration. You should treat yourself to a gift, go out to dinner with a friend, or do something else to congratulate yourself, because you've earned it.

Unfortunately, there are also times that you don't get the job. If you feel that the interview didn't go well, you probably won't be surprised at not receiving a job offer. But sometimes, even when the interview seems to have gone very well, you still find a rejection letter in the mail. What happened? You got along well with the interviewer. You talked about everything under the sun—films, hometowns, career goals, even the weather. Why didn't she make you an offer?

Sometimes interviews seem to go well when, in fact, they really haven't gone well at all. You should beware of the interview that gets too chummy. It may be that the interviewer has already decided not to hire you and out of politeness spends the remaining time talking about everything but you.

The simple truth is that most initial interviews really last only about 5 minutes. The actual interview always takes longer—20 minutes, 30 minutes, sometimes even an hour. But if you haven't convinced the interviewer by the 5-minute point that you're the right person for the job, it will be next to impossible to recover. Recoveries do happen, but they're rare.

In that first 5 minutes of the interview, the interviewer will already know almost everything he or she wants to know about you. Your appearance. Your grooming. Your handshake. Your personal presence. Your eye contact. Your articulation. And, most important, your personality. Notice that there's no mention here of your experience, knowledge, education, or talent. As mentioned earlier, those are the things that got you to the interview in the first place. It's the kind of person you are, or appear to be, that will take you to the next level.

If you get a rejection letter, it's important for you to remember that it doesn't mean that there's something wrong with you. Interviewers generally know the kind of person they're looking for, the kind of person who will reflect well on them and will fit in with their team, and it may be that you're just not that kind of person. But it doesn't mean that another interviewer might not have exactly the opposite reaction. You can't give up. *You have to keep trying.*

You should, of course, also learn from the experience. Evaluate your performance. Did I say something I shouldn't have? Did I neglect to say something I should have? Did I forget to polish my shoes? Did I forget to maintain eye contact? If you realize that you did any of these things during the interview, you'll be aware of them and make every effort to avoid doing them the next time.

Another way to learn from the experience is to call the interviewer and ask why you didn't get the job. This can be a difficult call to make, but if you can bring yourself to do it, you should. When you get the interviewer on the phone, be friendly. Thank her for giving you the opportunity to meet her, say you're sorry that you weren't right for the job, and ask if she could provide you with any feedback that will help in future job interviews. Listen to what she has to say. Before you hang up, ask if you can stay in touch by sending updates on your career. After all, you are freelancing, and you need to keep those contacts. Chances are she'll accept this. Just make sure that you do keep in touch, and send her another thank-you letter.

INTERVIEW CHECKLIST

This is what everything else has been leading up to, where all your hard work pays off: your first interview for a real job in the film industry. It's also your opportunity to shine and to show a film professional that you have what it takes to have a successful career in the movie business. This list will serve to remind you of the steps you must take to prepare yourself for that all-important interview.

1. The key element to successful interviewing can be summed up in one word: attitude. Although other applicants for this position may have more experience, more knowledge, and even more talent, if you demonstrate a truly positive attitude you'll be a front-runner for the job.

2. Like an actor or actress preparing for an audition, you have to learn your lines and practice your skills. Have at least one rehearsal interview—and preferably more—with someone who will provide you with constructive criticism on your interviewing skills. If you can, videotape the rehearsals so you can critique your own performance, and keep practicing until you feel that you've got it right.

3. Find out as much as you can about the interviewer and the production company or studio he or she works for. Use your contacts to gather this information or to find people who can provide you with the information. The more knowledgeable you are about the interviewer and the company, the better your chances are of getting the job.

4. Be sure to wear neat, clean, and appropriate clothing to the interview. If you're not sure about what's appropriate, ask someone who knows. Don't forget about your shoes, because some interviewers pay attention to what's on your feet.

5. Interviews are about communication, but you don't only communicate with words. Body language counts too, and there are dos and don'ts in interviewing that you should always remember. Do make eye contact, exhibit appropriate facial expressions, sit and stand up tall, gesture in a natural manner, and maintain your personal space while respecting the personal space of the interviewer. Don't behave in a manner that will make the interviewer think you are nervous, untrustworthy, or defensive.

6. Believe in yourself, and act as though you do. Don't be afraid to sell yourself, because if you don't, no one else will. Self-confidence, as long as it's not overdone, is a trait that appeals to interviewers.

7. As early as possible in the interview, ask the interviewer to tell you about the position and about what kind of person he is looking for. Having this information will enable you to tailor your answers to make it clear that your skills and abilities will meet the interviewer's needs.

8. At entry-level positions in the film business, salary isn't really negotiable. If you're a union member, your wages have already been determined by agreement between the union and the employers. In nonunion positions, employers are doing you a favor by hiring you, so you should be grateful for whatever they offer.

9. Always remember to send a thank-you note to the interviewer as soon as possible after your meeting. Many people don't bother to do this, and—all things being equal—writing a note can tip the balance in your favor when the interviewer makes a hiring decision.

10. The first 5 minutes of an interview are the ones that really count. If you haven't impressed the interviewer by then, chances are you never will. To make sure that you make the best impression possible, go back over all the suggestions in this chapter just before you set out for the interview.

11. If you get the job, treat yourself to a celebration. You've earned it. If you don't, don't give up. There are other, maybe even better, jobs out there, and if you persevere you'll get one of them. In the meantime, learn what you can from your experience: critique your own performance and call the interviewer to ask if he or she can offer any helpful hints for future interviews.

chapter 10

It's a Wrap

To behind-the-scenes film workers, "It's a wrap" is a simultaneously joyful and daunting expression to hear. It's joyful because it means the film production is over and, after all their hard work, they'll get to have some time off, at least until the next gig. It's daunting because they may not know when or where that next gig might be. Ultimately, that's what the business always boils down to: your next job. If you don't have another job lined up, it's time to go out and hustle for one.

For you, the problem of finding that next job is there, but it's just over the horizon. Making a career in the film industry is a long journey, but at this point you're just about to take the first step. The purpose of this book has been to help you take that step—to start you on what will hopefully be a long and fruitful career in the movies. In the meantime, there are a few things that you should keep in mind, both now and in the future.

EVERYONE STARTS AT THE BOTTOM

Your love of films has brought you to the point of wanting a career in the movies. But you have to be prepared to start at the bottom, because that's where everyone starts. Although ultimately you may be able to make a substantial living, right now you have to be willing to work hard for little or no money. The important thing now is to get experience. That experience will help you get the job you really want later on.

Right now, and in the future, you have to keep your ultimate goal in mind. Don't let the low salary and long hours get you down. Focus on the rewards of the work even during the tough times. Remember that even if you're working as a go-fer or a production assistant, you're still part of the team, part of the filmmaking process. Someday you just might see your name in credits on the big screen.

IT'S ALL ABOUT COMMUNICATION

Ultimately, what films are really about is communicating through a visual medium. But long before the cameras start rolling, long before there's a single director, actor, or behind-the-scenes person hired, there's a lot of communication that's done on paper. If you want to have a successful career in the film industry, it's necessary that you learn to communicate well in writing.

That means creating and maintaining a well-written and professional-looking resume. It also means writing clear and concise cover letters, networking letters, follow-up letters, and thank-you notes. You'll have to do this not only to get a job, but also to let someone know that you appreciate being hired, and, after a production has wrapped, to tell them that you appreciated the work.

NETWORKING IS THE KEY

Although there are obviously many full-time jobs in the film industry, a large percentage of those who work in the business do it on a freelance basis. It can be a precarious way of making a living, but if you can handle it there are many rewards. In order to get that first job, though, as well as every job in the future, you're going to have to build up and maintain as extensive a network as you possibly can.

You've already learned how to begin that process, but the important thing to remember is that it's a process that never ends. Not only do you have to develop a network of contacts in the business, but you also have to maintain all those contacts while, at the same time, you add new ones.

The contact who can't help you now might very well refer you to a job next month, or even hire you for one a year from now. There are hundreds of thousands of people working in the movie business, but it's still ultimately a small community. And it's who you know that gets you where you want to go.

It's also important to remember the people who've helped you along the way. These people are special. They didn't have to take time from their work to show you the ropes. They did it because somewhere in their career someone helped them, and they wanted to return or pass on the favor, just as you will one day.

STAY IN THE KNOW

Movies are one of the few industries that depend largely on new products. "Yes, Mr. Cameron," the public says, "*Titanic* was a fantastic movie, but what are you doing now?" For that reason, there are new things being done, new projects being developed, and new stars—both in front of and behind the cameras—being born every day. If you don't keep up with what's happening, you're going to be left behind.

It's essential that you do all you can to make sure you know what's going on in the industry. This means you have to read the industry's trade papers and magazines religiously. Join groups, take seminars, and attend film festivals. You also have to learn how to use the Internet and every other available source of information on what's happening in the film business.

ALWAYS BE PROFESSIONAL

You may not be a film professional now, but if you don't start acting like one from the beginning, you never will be. Because it's an incredibly competitive business, no one has any time for people who are anything less than complete professionals.

That means, first of all, that you have to be able to get along with people. A film is a cooperative venture, so no matter what field of the industry you choose to go into, you're always going to be a member of a team. No one likes to work with unpleasant people—even popular actors have seen their careers go into decline because they developed reputations for being difficult. Obviously, no one gets along with everybody, but if you don't always behave in a professional manner, you may wake up one morning and find that you no longer have job prospects.

It also means that you always have to do as good a job as you're capable of doing. Again, because of all the competition in the business, there's always someone waiting in the wings to take your job if you don't do it well. None of us can be perfect all the time, but it's essential that you always strive for excellence, because if you don't even try to be the best you'll never be able to achieve it.

Finally, you always have to look your best. As a behind-the-scenes worker, you don't have to be as handsome as an actor or as beautiful as an actress, but you do have to be presentable. It may be fine to wear a pair of torn jeans and an old shirt once you've become a sought-after cinematographer, film editor, or whatever, but on your way up you can't afford to stand out for anything other than your talent.

Working in the film industry isn't for everyone. It's only for those who have a passion for playing a part in the filmmaking process and are willing to do what has to be done to play that part. Disappointments can break your heart, and new opportunities can bring you to the heights of ecstasy. The industry demands long hours and hard efforts, but the work is exciting and exhilarating.

Ultimately, the most important thing, the thing that drives people to careers in film, is that movies are *magical*. For as long as you can remember, you've sat in darkened movie theaters, watched in fascination as figures moved across the screen, and wondered what it would be like to be part of that magic. And now you can be part of this fascinating and challenging world. It's up to you.

Break a leg!

appendix 1

Key Employers and Film Commission Offices

FILM PRODUCTION COMPANIES

ABC Pictures
2020 Avenue of the Stars, 5th Floor
Los Angeles, California 90067
Telephone: 310-557-6806
Fax: 310-557-6021
Key Employees:
Didier Pietri, Sr. VP
Dennis Brown, VP, Production
Darren Frankel, Exec. Dir., Post Production
Brian Colgan, Mgr., Business Affairs

American Zoetrope
916 Kearny Street
San Francisco, California 94133
Telephone: 415-788-7500; 310-385-4218
Fax: 415-989-7910; 310-385-4204
Web Page: http://www.zoetrope.com
Key Employees:
Fred Fuchs, President
Tom Luddy, Producer
Genevieve Haag, Asst. to Mr. Fuchs
Shannon Lail, Asst. to Francis Coppola

aMuse Productions
10900 Wilshire Boulevard, Suite 950
Los Angeles, California 90024
Telephone: 310-209-6155
Fax: 310-209-6160
Key Employees:
Gary Adelson, Producer
Valerie Letton, Exec. Asst. to Gary Adelson

Artisan Entertainment
2700 Colorado Avenue, 2nd Floor
Santa Monica, California 90404
Telephone: 310-449-9200; 212-577-2400
Fax: 310-255-3920; 310-255-3970
E-mail: name@live-entertainment.com
Key Employees:
Bill Block, President
Amir Malin, President
Meltem Demirer, Dir., Production/Finance
Leilani Forby, Dir., Production/Acquisitions
Beck Sloca, Mgr., Business Affairs
Cybelle Greenman, Mgr., Development/Production
Dana Reid, Mgr., Development/Production

Beacon Pictures
Care of: Warner-Hollywood Studios
1041 North Formosa Avenue
Hollywood, California 90046-6798
Telephone: 213-850-2651
Fax: 213-850-2613
Key Employees:
Armyan Bernstein, Chairman
Marc Abraham, President
Thomas Bliss, COO/Exec. VP
Merry Rose, Mgr., Human Resources
Katherine Bishop, Asst. to Mr. Bliss
A. B. Fischer, 2nd Asst. to Mr. Bernstein
Misty Green, Asst. to Mr. Abraham

Blue Relief, Inc.
500 South Buena Vista Street, Animation 1C6
Burbank, California 91521-1620
Telephone: 818-560-2255
Fax: 818-567-4092
E-mail: bluerelief@aol.com
Key Employees:
Diane Keaton, Director/Producer/Actor
Bill Robinson, Producer
Laura Citrano, Asst. to Diane Keaton
Emily Lenzner, Asst. to Bill Robinson

Broadway Pictures (LA)
  Care of: Paramount Studios
  5555 Melrose Avenue, Dressing Rm #109
  Los Angeles, California 90038-3197
  Telephone: 213-956-5729
  Fax: 213-862-8605
  Key Employees:
  Lorne Michaels, Chairman
  Bob Weiss, President (213-956-5729)
  Carr D'Angelo, VP, Production
  Kyu Kahn, Asst. to Bob Weiss

C/W Productions
  5555 Melrose Avenue
  Hollywood, California 90038
  Telephone: 213-956-8150
  Fax: 213-862-1250
  Key Employees:
  Paula Wagner, Partner/Producer
  Jonathan Sanger, Producer
  Ryan Warren, Producer's Assistant

Castle Rock Entertainment
  335 North Maple Drive, Suite 135
  Beverly Hills, California 90210-3867
  Telephone: 310-285-2300
  Fax: 310-285-2345
  Web Page: http://www.castle-rock.com
  Key Employees:
  Alan Horn, Chairman/CEO
  Rob Reiner, Producer/Director
  Andrew Scheinman, Producer/Director
  Martin Shafer, Pres., Castle Rock Pictures
  Liz Glotzer, Pres., Production, Castle Rock Pictures
  Jeffrey Stott, Exec. VP, Production Management
  Jess Wittenberg, Exec. VP
  Carlos Perez, VP, Administration
  Sharon Lignier, Dir., Business Affairs Administration

CinePoint Productions, Inc.
111 North Sepulveda Boulevard, Suite 250
Manhattan Beach, California 90266
Telephone: 310-937-1535
Fax: 310-798-9443
E-mail: cinepoint@worldnet.att.net
Key Employees:
Michael Russell, Co-President
Stephen LoCascio, Co-President

Columbia Pictures
10202 West Washington Boulevard
Culver City, California 90232-3195
Telephone: 310-244-4000
Fax: 310-244-2626
Web Page: http://www.spe.sony.com/
Key Employees:
Christopher Lee, Pres., Production
Amy Baer, Exec. VP, Production
Bryan Lee, Exec. VP, Business Affairs and Operations
Mark B. Horowitz, VP, Business Affairs Administration
Thomas Stack, VP, Business Affairs and Contract Administration
Ricky Strauss, VP, Production
Mark Wyman, VP, Business Affairs

Dimension Films
Care of: Miramax Films
375 Greenwich Street
New York, New York 10013-2338
Telephone: 212-941-3800; 213-951-4200
Fax: 212-941-3949; 213-951-4218
Web Page: http://www.dimensionfilms.com
Key Employees:
Bob Weinstein, Co-Chairman (NY)
Cary Granat, President (NY)
Richard Potter, Sr. VP, Production and Development (NY)
Andrew Rona, Sr. VP, Production and Development (NY)
Cary Meadow, VP, Business Affairs

DreamWorks SKG
100 Universal Plaza, Building 10
Universal City, California 91608-1085
Telephone: 818-733-7000
Key Employees:
David Geffen, Administration
Jeffrey Katzenberg, Administration
Steven Spielberg, Administration
Helene Hahn, Administration
Ron Nelson, Administration
Art Frazier, Business Affairs

H2 Productions
212 San Vicente Boulevard, Suite H
Santa Monica, California 90402
Telephone: 310-839-7927
Fax: 310-394-6510
Key Employees:
Steven Bakalar, Producer/Writer
Devorah Cutler-Rubenstein, Producer/Writer/Director

Harpo Films, Inc.
345 North Maple Drive, Suite 315
Beverly Hills, California 90210
Telephone: 310-278-5559
Key Employees:
Oprah Winfrey, Chairman/CEO
Jeffrey Jacobs, President
Kate Forte, Exec. VP, Development and Production
Tim Tortora, Dir., Production
Stephanie Harris, Exec. Assistant/Office Mgr.

HBO Pictures
2049 Century Park East, Suite 3600
Los Angeles, California 90067-3215
Telephone: 310-201-9200
Web Page: http://www.hbo.com
Key Employees:
John Matoian, President (310-201-9405)
Glenn Whitehead, VP, Business Affairs and Production (310-201-9291)
Suzanne Young, VP, Business Affairs (310-201-9353)
Carrie Frazier, VP, Talent and Casting (310-201-9537)
Ellen Rudolph, Dir., Operations (310-201-9549)
Donna Pearlmutter, Production Supervisor (310-201-9464)

Jim Henson Pictures
5358 Melrose Avenue, Suite 300W
Hollywood, California 90038
Telephone: 213-960-4096
Fax: 213-960-4780
Web Page: http://www.henson.com
Key Employees:
Stephanie Allain, Pres., Production
Kristine Belson, Production
Louis M. Phillips, Production/Administration
Tom Supa, Asst. to Ms. Allain

Ignite Entertainment
225 Arizona Avenue, Suite 250
Santa Monica, California 90401
Telephone: 310-458-5256
Fax: 310-458-3792
Web Page: http://www.hsx.com
Key Employees:
Michael Burns, Chairman
Leanna Creel, Pres., Production
Marc Butan, VP, Business Affairs
Leon Marucci, Asst. to Leanna Creel

Illusion Entertainment Group
201 Santa Monica Boulevard, Suite 625
Santa Monica, California 90401
Telephone: 310-458-7747
Fax: 310-458-1597
Key Employees:
Oliver Stone, Writer/Director/Producer
Dan Halsted, President
Katherine Ku, Exec. Asst. to Dan Halsted
Rob Wilson, Exec. Asst. to Oliver Stone
Becky Kuhns, Asst. to Oliver Stone
Rick Lubaroff, Asst. to Dan Halsted

Imagine Entertainment
    1925 Century Park East, Suite 2300
    Los Angeles, California 90067-2734
    Telephone: 310-277-1665
    Fax: 310-785-0107
    Key Employees:
    Brian Grazer, Co-Chairman
    Ron Howard, Co-Chairman
    Karen Kehela, Co-Chairman, Imagine Films
    Michael Bostick, President, Imagine Films
    Robin Barris, Sr. VP, Administration and Operations

Kennedy/Marshall Company
    1351 4th Street, 4th Floor
    Santa Monica, California 90401
    Telephone: 310-656-8400
    Fax: 310-656-8430
    Key Employees:
    Kathleen Kennedy, Producer
    Frank Marshall, Producer/Director

Maple Palm Productions
    429 Santa Monica Boulevard, Suite 500
    Santa Monica, California 90401
    Telephone: 310-458-8163
    Fax: 310-451-9754
    E-mail: mpalm@ix.netcom.com
    Key Employees:
    Dave Thomas, Chairman
    Bill Bromiley, President
    Jonathan Josell, VP, Production
    Mark Barbolak, VP

Merchant-Ivory
    250 West 57th Street, Suite 1913A
    New York, New York 10107
    Telephone: 212-582-8049
    Fax: 212-459-9201
    Key Employees:
    Ismail Merchant, Co-President/Producer
    James Ivory, Co-President/Director
    Dara McQuillan, Production Supervisor/Asst. to President
    Marla L. Shelton, Production Supervisor/Asst. to President

Mirage Enterprises
Care of: Sony Pictures Entertainment
10202 West Washington Boulevard, Lean Building
Culver City, California 90232-3195
Telephone: 310-244-2044
Fax: 310-244-0044
Key Employees:
Sydney Pollack, Producer/Director
William Horberg, Producer
David Rubin, Producer
Jenny McLaren, Office Manager
Donna Ostroff, Asst. to Mr. Pollack

Miramax Films
Care of: Tribeca Film Center
375 Greenwich Street
New York, New York 10013-2338
Telephone: 212-941-3800; 213-951-4200
Fax: 212-941-3949; 213-951-4211
Web Page: http://www.miramax.com
Key Employees:
Harvey Weinstein, Co-Chairman (NY)
Bob Weinstein, Co-Chairman (NY)
Mark Gill, President, Miramax LA
Amy Slotnick, Dir., Production/Casting (NY)

Moonstone Entertainment
335 North Maple Drive, Suite 222
Beverly Hills, California 90210
Telephone: 310-247-6060
Fax: 310-247-6061
Key Employees:
Ernst Etchie Stroh, President
Yael Stroh, Exec. VP

Morgan Creek Prods.
4000 Warner Boulevard, Building 76
Burbank, California 91522
Telephone: 818-954-4800
Fax: 818-954-4811
Key Employees:
James G. Robinson, Chairman/CEO
Jonathan A. Zimbert, President, Production

Muse Productions, Inc.
15 Brooks Avenue, Unit B
Venice, California 90291
Telephone: 310-306-2001
Fax: 310-574-2614
E-mail: musefilm@aol.com
Key Employees:
Chris Hanley, President/Producer
Jordan Gertner, VP/Producer

New Line Cinema
116 North Robertson Boulevard, Suite 200
Los Angeles, California 90048
Telephone: 310-854-5811; 212-649-4900
Fax: 310-854-1824; 212-649-4966
Web Page: http://www.newline.com
Key Employees:
Robert Shaye, Chairman/CEO, New Line Cinema (NY and LA)
Michael Lynne, Pres./COO, New Line Cinema (NY)
Lynn Harris, Exec. VP, Production
Ben Zinkin, Exec. VP, Business Affairs
Sara Frith, VP, Business Affairs

New Regency Productions
4000 Warner Boulevard, Building 66
Burbank, California 91522-0001
Telephone: 818-954-3044
Fax: 818-954-3295
Web Page: http://www.newregency.com
Key Employees:
Arnon Milchan, Producer
Bridget Johnson, President, Production
David Matalon, President/CEO
Patrick Crowley, Exec. VP, Production
Carole Nix, Production Supervisor

Paramount Pictures—Motion Picture Group
5555 Melrose Avenue
Los Angeles, California 90038-3197
Telephone: 323-956-5000
Web Page: http://www.paramount.com
Key Employees:
Sherry Lansing, Chairman, Motion Picture Group
Robert G. Friedman, Vice Chairman, Motion Picture Group
John Goldwyn, President, Paramount Motion Pictures

Phoenician Films

8228 Sunset Boulevard, Suite 311
Los Angeles, California 90046
Telephone: 213-848-3444
Fax: 213-848-9612
Key Employees:
Elie Samaha, Chairman
Tia Carrere, President
Paul D. Brown, Executive Assistant
Malee Nerenhausen, Executive Assistant

Propaganda Films

940 North Mansfield Avenue
Los Angeles, California 90038-3197
Telephone: 213-462-6400
Fax: 213-463-7874
Key Employees:
Steve Golin, Chairman
James Tauber, President/COO
Tim Clawson, Head, Production

Red Hour Films

193 North Roberston Boulevard
Beverly Hills, California 90211
Telephone: 310-289-2565
Fax: 310-289-5988
Key Employees:
Ben Stiller, Filmmaker/Actor
George Linardos, Producer
Erin Alexander, Asst. to Ben Stiller

Storm Entertainment

225 Santa Monica Boulevard, Suite 601
Santa Monica, California 90401
Telephone: 310-656-2500
Fax: 310-656-2510
E-mail: storment95@aol.com
Key Employee:
H. Michael Heuser, President/CEO

Trimark Pictures
2644 30th Street
Santa Monica, California 90405-3009
Telephone: 310-314-2000
Fax: 310-399-8246
E-mail: trimark@trimarkpictures.com
Web Page: http://www.trimarkpictures.com
Key Employees:
Mark Amin, Chairman/CEO
James Keegan, Sr. VP/CFO
Cami Winikoff, Exec. VP/Chief Administrative Officer
Jonathon Komack Martin, Exec. VP, Production
Wayne Levin, Dir., Business Affairs
Donna Solomon, Mgr., Production

Turner Original Productions
1050 Techwood Drive NW
Atlanta, Georgia 30318
Telephone: 404-827-2047
Fax: 404-885-4433
Web Page: http://www.turner.com
Key Employees:
Pat Mitchell, Pres., Turner Original Prods.
Teya Ryan, Sr. VP and Exec. Producer (CNN)
Vivian Schiller, Sr. VP/General Manager
Jacoba Atlas, VP/Supervising Producer (LA)
Louis Lettes, VP, Business Affairs (404-885-0916)
Tom McMahon, VP/Supervising Producer (LA)
John Savage, VP/Supervising Producer (Atlanta)
Tracy McArdle, Talent and Development Executive (LA)
Dan McKenzie, Exec. Asst. to Ms. Atlas and Mr. McMahon (LA)
Julie Bitton, Asst. to Ms. Schiller
Ann Howard, Asst. to Pat Mitchell

Twentieth Century Fox
10201 West Pico Boulevard
Los Angeles, California 90035
Telephone: 310-369-1000
Web Page: http://www.fox.com
Key Employees:
William Mechanic, Chairman/CEO
Thomas Sherak, Chair., 20th Domestic Film Group/Sr. EVP, Fox Films
Steven Bersch, Exec. VP, Business Affairs
Daniel Ferleger, Sr. VP, Business Affairs
Mark Resnick, Sr. VP, Business Affairs
Stephen Plum, VP, Business Affairs
Victoria Rossellini, VP, Business Affairs
Serena Westwell, Exec. Dir., Talent Relations

Twentieth Century Fox—Fox 2000 (LA)
10201 West Pico Boulevard, Building 78
Los Angeles, California 90035
Telephone: 310-369-2041
Fax: 310-369-4258
Web Page: http://www.fox.com
Key Employees:
Laura Ziskin, President
Kevin McCormick, Exec. VP, Production
Alex Gartner, Exec. VP, Production
Carla Hacken, Sr. VP
Jack Leslie, Dir., Development
Lisa Harrison, Talent Development and Relations Executive
Chris Rico, 1st Asst. to Laura Ziskin
Lea Oggs, 2nd Asst. to Laura Ziskin
Nancy Covello, Asst. to Kevin McCormick
Laura Williams, Asst. to J. Leslie

Twentieth Century Fox—Searchlight Pictures
10201 West Pico Boulevard, Building 38
Los Angeles, California 90035
Telephone: 310-369-4402; 212-556-8245
Fax: 310-369-2359; 212-556-8248
Web Page: http://www.fox.com
Key Employees:
Lindsay Law, President
Joseph De Marco, Exec. VP
Claudia Lewis, Sr. VP, Production
Joe Pichirallo, VP, Production
J. Michael Stremel, Dir., Production (NY)

United Artists Pictures
> 2500 Broadway Street, 5th Floor
> Santa Monica, California 90404-3061
> Telephone: 310-449-3000
> Web Page: http://www.mgmua.com
> Key Employees:
> Frank Mancuso, CEO/Chairman of the Board
> Lindsay Doran, President
> James Middleton, VP, Production and Development

Universal Pictures
> 100 Universal City Plaza
> Universal City, California 91608-1085
> Telephone: 818-777-1000
> Web Page: http://www.universalstudios.com
> Key Employees:
> Casey Silver, Chairman
> Chris McGurk, President/COO
> Jon Gumpert, Executive VP
> Bahman Naraghi, Sr. VP, Planning and Operations
> James M. Horowitz, VP, Business Affairs

Walt Disney Pictures/Touchstone Pictures
> 500 South Buena Vista Street
> Burbank, California 91521-0001
> Telephone: 818-560-1000
> Web Page: http://www.disney.com
> Key Employees:
> Joe Roth, Chairman, Walt Disney Studios
> Richard W. Cook, Chairman, Walt Disney Motion Pictures Group
> Donald DeLine, President, Touchstone Pictures
> David E. Vogel, President, Walt Disney Pictures
> Chris Floyd, VP, Business Affairs
> Steven W. Gerse, VP, Business Affairs

Warner Bros. Pictures
4000 Warner Boulevard
Burbank, California 91522-0001
Telephone: 818-954-6000
Web Page: http://www.warnerbros.com
Key Employees:
Robert A. Daly, Chairman/Co-CEO
Terry Semel, Chairman/Co-CEO

FILM COMMISSION OFFICES

Alaska Film Commission
Alaska Film Office
Division of Tourism
Mary Pignalberi, Director
3601 C Street, Suite 700
Anchorage, Alaska 99503
Phone: 907-269-8137
Alternate: 907-562-4163
Fax: 907-269-8136

Alabama Film Commission
A Division of Alabama Development Office
State of Alabama
401 Adams Avenue
Montgomery, Alabama 36130
Telephone: 800-633-5898
Alternate: 334-242-4195
Fax: 334-242-2077

Arkansas Film Commission
Arkansas Motion Picture Development Office
Prisca Hohnbaum
One State Capitol Mall, Suite 2C-200
Little Rock, Arkansas 72201
Telephone: 501-682-7676
Fax: 501-682-3456
Web Page: http://www.aidc.state.ar.us

Arizona Film Commission
Linda Peterson Warren, Director
3800 North Central Avenue, Building D
Phoenix, Arizona 85212
Telephone: 800-523-6695
Alternate: 602-280-1380
Fax: 602-280-1384

California Film Commission
Patti Stolkin Archuletta, Director
7080 Hollywood Boulevard, Suite 900
Hollywood, California 90028
Telephone: 800-858-4749
Alternate: 213-860-2960
Fax: 213-860-2972
E-mail: filmca@aol.com

Colorado Film Commission
Colorado Motion Picture and Television Commission
Michael D. Klein, Director
1625 Broadway, Suite 1700
Denver, Colorado 80202
Telephone: 800-726-8887
Alternate: 303-620-4500
Fax: 303-620-4545
E-mail: staff@coloradofilm.org
Web Page: http://www.coloradofilm.org

Connecticut Film Commission
Connecticut Dept. of Economic Development
Tourism Division
Bert Brown, Director
865 Brook Street
Rocky Hill, Connecticut 06067-3405
Telephone: 800-392-2122 (Business Response Center)

District of Columbia Film Commission
Mayor's Office of Motion Picture and TV
717 14th Street NW, 12th Floor
Washington, DC 20005
Telephone: 202-727-6608
Alternate: 202-727-6607

The Florida Entertainment Commission
505 17th Street
Miami, Florida 33139
Telephone: 305-673-7468 (Miami)
Alternate: 818-777-1613 (Los Angeles)
Fax: 305-673-7168

Georgia Film Commission
Georgia Film and Videotape Office
Norman Bielowicz, Director
285 Peachtree Center Avenue, NE
Marquis Tower II, Suite 1000
Atlanta, Georgia 30303
Telephone: 404-656-3591
Fax: 404-651-9063
Web Page: http://www.telefilm-south.com/Georgia/Georgia.html

Hawaii Film Commission
Georgette T. Deemer, Director
P.O. Box 2359
Honolulu, Hawaii 96804
Telephone: 808-586-2570
Fax: 808-586-2572
E-mail: gdeemer@pixi.com

Idaho Film Bureau
Peg Owens, Director
700 West State Street, 2nd Floor
P.O. Box 83720
Boise, Idaho 83720-0093
Telephone: 800-942-8338
Alternate: 208-334-2470
Fax: 203:334-2631
E-mail: powens@idoc.state.id.us
Web Page: http://www.idoc.state.id.us/film/idaho

Illinois Film Commission
Ron Ver Kuilen, Director
100 West Randolph Street
Suite 3-400
Chicago, Illinois 60601
Telephone: 312-814-3600
Fax: 312-814-8874

Indiana Film Commission
Indiana Department of Commerce
Jane Rulon, Director
One North Capitol Avenue, Suite 700
Indianapolis, Indiana 46204-2288
Telephone: 317-232-8829
Fax: 317-233-6887
E-mail: jrulon@commerce.state.in.us
Web Page: http://www.a1.com/derringer/filmcomm.html

Iowa Film Commission
Iowa Department of Economic Development
Wendol M. Jarvis, Director
200 East Grand Avenue
Des Moines, Iowa 50309
Telephone: 515-242-4726
Alternate: 515-242-4757 (Action Line)
Fax: 515-242-4859
E-mail: paul.frank@ided.state.ia.us
Web Page: http://www.state.ia.us/film

Kansas Film Commission
Kansas Department of Commerce and Housing
Travel and Tourism Development Division
Vicky Henley, Manager
700 Southwest Harrison Street, Suite 1300
Topeka, Kansas 66603-3712
Telephone: 913-296-4927
Fax: 913-296-6988
E-mail: jconrad@ink.org

Kentucky Office of Motion Picture Services
Jim Toole, Director of Motion Picture Services
Capital Plaza Tower
500 Mero Street, Suite 2200
Frankfort, Kentucky 40601
Telephone: 800-345-6591 (800-FILM KY 1)
Alternate: 502-564-3456 (502-564-FILM)
Web Page: http://www.telefilm-south.com/KY/KYLG/KFC.html

Maine Film Office
D. Lea Girardin, Director
State House Station 59
Augusta, Maine 04333-0059
Telephone: 207-287-5703
Alternate: 207-287-5705 (24-Hour Message Line)
Fax: 207-287-8070
E-mail: gregory.d.gadberry@state.me.us
Web Page: http://www.state.me.us/decd/film

Maryland Film Commission
Michael B. Styer, Director
217 East Redwood Street, 9th Floor
Baltimore, Maryland 21202
Telephone: 800-333-6632
Alternate: 410-767-6340
Fax: 410-333-0044

Massachusetts Film Office
Robin Dawson, Director
Ten Park Plaza, Suite 2310
Boston, Massachusetts 02116
Telephone: 617-973-8800
Fax: 617-973-8810
E-mail: film@state.ma.us
Web Page: http://www.magnet.state.ma.us/film

Michigan Film Commission
Michigan Film Office
Janet Lockwood, Director
201 North Washington Square
Victor Centre, 2nd Floor
Lansing, Michigan 48913
Telephone: 800-477-3456
Alternate: 517-373-0638
Fax: 517-241-0593
Web Page: http://www.state.mi.us/mjc/ceo/

Minnesota Film Board
Kelly "K2" Heikkila, Director of Production
401 North Third Street, Suite 460
Minneapolis, Minnesota 55401
Telephone: 612-332-6493
Fax: 612-332-3735
E-mail: infor@mnfilm.org
Web Page: http://www.mnfilm.org

Mississippi Film Office
Ward Emling, Director
P.O. Box 849
Jackson, Mississippi 39205-0849
Telephone: 601-359-3297
Alternate: 601-359-2112 (Production Hotline)
Fax: 601-359-5757
E-mail: wemling%gw@decd.state.ms.us
Web Page: http://www.decd.state.ms.us/FILM/FILM.HTM

Missouri Film Commission
Robyne Collier, Production Specialist
301 West High Street, Room 720
P.O. Box 118
Jefferson City, Missouri 65201
Telephone: 573-751-9050
Fax: 573-751-7384
E-mail: rcollier@mail.state.mo.us
Web page: http://www.ecodev.state.mo.us/film

Montana Film Commission
Department of Commerce
Lonie Stimac, Director
1424 9th Avenue
P.O. Box 200533
Helena, Montana 59620-0533
Telephone: 800-553-4563
Alternate: 406-444-3762
Fax: 406-444-4191
E-mail: montanafilm@travel.state.mt.us
Web Page: montanafilm.mt.state.mt.us

Nebraska Film Commission
Travel and Tourism Division
Department of Economic Development
Laurie J. Richards, Director
700 South 16th Street
P.O. Box 94666
Lincoln, Nebraska 68509-4666
Telephone: 800-228-4307
Alternate: 402-471-3680
Fax: 402-471-3026
E-mail: laurier@ded2.ded.state.ne.us
Web Page: http://www.film.ded.state.ne.us

Nevada Film Commission
Las Vegas Office
Bob Hirsch, Director
555 East Washington, Suite 5400
Las Vegas, Nevada 89101
Telephone: 702-486-2711
Fax: 702-486-2712
E-mail: danterh@aol.com
Web Page: http://www.intermind.net

New Hampshire Film Commission
Laura Simoes, Director
P.O. Box 1856
172 Pembroke Road
Concord, New Hampshire 03302-1856
Telephone: 603-271-2598
Fax: 603-271-2629
E-mail: ottd@dred.state.nh.us
Web Page: http://www.dred.state.nh.us

New Jersey Motion Picture and Television Commission
Joseph Friedman, Executive Director
P.O. Box 47023
153 Halsey Street, Fifth Floor
Newark, New Jersey 07101
Telephone: 973-648-6279
Fax: 973-648-7350
E-mail: njfilm@nj.com
Web Page: http://www.nj.com

New Mexico Film Commission
Linda Taylor Hutchison, Director
1050 Old Pesos Trail
Santa Fe, New Mexico 87503
Telephone: 800-545-9871
Alternate: 505-827-7365
Fax: 505-827-7369
Web Page: http://www.edd.state.nm.us/ED/divisions/film/film.htm

New York Film Commission
New York State Governor's Office/Motion Picture-TV Development
Pat Kaufman, Deputy Commissioner
633 Third Avenue, 33rd Floor
New York, New York 10017
Telephone: 212-803-2330
Fax: 212-803-2339
Web Page: http://www.empire.state.ny.us/

North Carolina Film Commission
Bill Arnold, Director
430 North Salisbury Street
Raleigh, North Carolina 27611
Telephone: 919-733-9900
Alternate: 800-232-9227 (Hotline)
Fax: 919-715-0151
Web Page: http://www.telefilm-south.com

North Dakota Film Commission
Pat Hertz, Film Commissioner
604 East Boulevard, 2nd Floor
Bismarck, North Dakota 58505-0825
Telephone: 800-328-2871
Alternate: 701-328-2874
Fax: 701-328-4878
E-mail: phertz@ranch.state.nd.us

Ohio Film Commission
Ohio Department of Development
Eve Lapolla, Director
77 South High Street, 29th Floor
P.O. Box 1001
Columbus, Ohio 43216
Telephone: 800-230-3523
Alternate: 614-466-2284
Fax: 614-466-6744
E-mail: elapolla@odod.ohio.gov
Web Page: http://www.ohiofilm.com

Oklahoma Film Commission
Robert M. Davis, Director
440 South Houston, Suite 304
Tulsa, Oklahoma 74127-8945
Telephone: 800-766-3456
Alternate: 918-581-2660
Fax: 918-581-2244

Oregon Film and Video Office
David Woolson, Director
121 SW Salmon Street, Suite 1205
Portland, Oregon 97204
Telephone: 503-229-5832
Fax: 503-229-6869
E-mail: shoot@oregonfilm.org
Web Page: http://www.oregonfilm.org

Pennsylvania Film Office
4th Floor—Forum Building
Harrisburg, Pennsylvania 17102
Telephone: 717-783-3456
Fax: 717-787-0687
Web Page: http://www.dced.state.pa.us

Rhode Island Film/TV Office
Rhode Island Economic Development Corporation
Rick Smith, Director
One West Exchange Street
Providence, Rhode Island 02903
Telephone: 401-277-3456
Fax: 401-273-8270
E-mail: rsmith@riedc.com
Web Page: http://www.riedc.com/rifilm/rifilmframe.html

South Carolina Film Office
South Carolina Deptartment of Parks, Recreation and Tourism
Isabel Hill, Director
Jeff Monkes
P.O. Box 7367
Columbia, South Carolina 29202
Telephone: 803-737-0490
Fax: 803-737-3104
E-mail: ihill@prt.state.sc.us
Web Page: http://www.telefilm-south.com/SC/SC.html

South Dakota Film Commission
Gary Keller, Director
711 East Wells Avenue
Pierre, South Dakota 57501-3369
Telephone: 800-952-3625
Alternate: 605-773-3301
Fax: 605-773-3256
E-mail: garyk@goed.state.sd.us
Web Page: http://www.state.sd.us

Tennessee Film, Entertainment and Music Commission
Anne Pope, Executive Director
320 Sixth Avenue North
Rachel Jackson Building—7th Floor
Nashville, Tennessee 37243-0790
Telephone: 800-251-8594
Alternate: 615-741-3456
Fax: 615-741-5554
Web Page: http://www.state.tn.us/film

Texas Film Commission
Tom Copeland, Director
P.O. Box 13246
Austin, Texas 78711
Telephone: 512-463-9200
Alternate: 512-463-7799 (production hotline)
Fax: 512-463-4114
E-mail: film@governor.state.tx.us
Web Page: http://www.governor.state.tx.us/film

Utah Film Commission
Leigh von der Esch, Executive Director
324 South State Street, Suite 500
Salt Lake City, Utah 84114-7330
Telephone: 800-453-8824
Alternate: 801-538-8740
Fax: 801-538-8886
E-mail: cemain.lvondere@state.ut.us
Web Page: http://www.ce.ex.state.ut.us/film/welcome.htm

Vermont Film Commission
Loranne Turgeon, Executive Director
10 Baldwin Street
P.O. Box 129
Montpelier, Vermont 05601
Telephone: 802-828-3618
Alternate: 802-828-3680 (hotline)
Fax: 802-828-2221
E-mail: vtfilmcom@dca.state.vt.us

Virginia Film Commission
Rita McClenny, Director
901 East Byrd Street
Richmond, Virginia 23219
Telephone: 804-371-8204; 800-854-6233
Alternate: 800-641-0810 (production hotline)
Fax: 804-371-8177
E-mail: vafilm@vedp.state.va.us
Web Page: http://www.film.virginia.org

Washington State Film Commission
Suzy Kellett, Director
2001 Sixth Avenue, Suite 2600
Seattle, Washington 98121
Telephone: 206-464-7148
Alternate: 206-464-6074 (Production Hotline)
Fax: 206-464-7722

West Virginia Film Commission
Mark McNabb, Director
West Virginia Development Office
Capitol Complex, Building 6, Room 525
Charleston, West Virginia 25305-0311
Telephone: 800-982-3386
Alternate: 304-558-2234
Fax: 304-558-1189

Wisconsin Film Office
Stanley Solheim, Director
201 West Washington Avenue
P.O. Box 7976
Madison, Wisconsin 53707-7976
Telephone: 800-345-6947
Fax: 608-266-3403
Web Page: http://www.film.state.wi.us

Wyoming Film Office
Michell Phelan, Director
Olivia Martinez, Admin. Asst.
1-25 at College Drive
Cheyenne, Wyoming 82002
Telephone: 800-458-6657
Alternate: 307-777-3400
Fax: 307-777-6904
E-mail: omarti@missc.state.wy.us
Web Page: http://www.commerce.state.wy.us/tourism/wfo/

appendix 2

Colleges and Universities That Offer Film Majors

The first list that follows includes colleges and universities that offer a major in Film/Cinema Studies. The second list includes colleges and universities that offer a major in Film-Video Making/Cinematography and Production. For both lists, when not apparent by name, state, province, or country locations are given. Two-year colleges are designated by an asterisk preceding the name.

Film/Cinema Studies
Academy of Art College (CA)
* Allan Hancock College (CA)
American University (DC)
Art Center College of Design (CA)

Bard College (NY)
Bennington College (VT)
Biola University (CA)
Boston University
Bowling Green State University (OH)
Brigham Young University (UT)
Brock University (ON)
Brooklyn College of the City University of New York
Brown University (RI)
Burlington College (VT)

California College of Arts and Crafts
California Institute of the Arts
California State University, Long Beach
California State University, Northridge
Calvin College (MI)
Carleton University (ON)
Carson-Newman College (TN)
Centenary College of Louisiana
Chapman University (CA)
Claremont McKenna College (CA)
Clark University (MA)

* Cochise College (AZ)
College of Santa Fe (NM)
College of Southeastern Europe (Greece)
College of Staten Island of the City University of New York
The Colorado College
Columbia College (IL)
Columbia College (NY)
Columbia College–Hollywood (CA)
Columbia University, School of General Studies (NY)
Concordia University (QB)
Curry College (MA)

* De Anza College (CA)
Denison University (OH)

Edinboro University of Pennsylvania
Emerson College (MA)
Emory University (GA)
The Evergreen State College (WA)

Fairleigh Dickinson University, Florham-Madison Campus (NJ)
Fairleigh Dickinson University, Teaneck-Hackensack Campus (NJ)
Florida Metropolitan University–Fort Lauderdale College
Florida State University
Fordham University (NY)
Franklin and Marshall College (PA)

Grand Valley State University (MI)

Hampshire College (MA)
Harvard University (MA)
Hofstra University (NY)
Hollins University (VA)
Howard University (DC)
Hunter College of the City University of New York

Indiana State University
Indiana University South Bend
Iona College (NY)
Ithaca College (NY)

Johns Hopkins University (MD)

Keene State College (NH)

* Lansing Community College (MI)
La Salle University (PA)
Laurentian University (ON)

* Long Beach City College (CA)
Long Island University, C.W. Post Campus (NY)
Long Island University, Southampton College, Friends World Program (NY)
* Los Angeles Valley College

Maharishi University of Management (IA)
Marlboro College (VT)
* Miami-Dade Community College (FL)
Middlebury College (VT)
Middle Tennessee State University
* Milwaukee Area Technical College
* Moorpark College (CA)
Mount Holyoke College (MA)

New Jersey City University
New York University
North Carolina School of the Arts
Northern Michigan University
Northwestern University (IL)

The Ohio State University
Ohio University
Olivet Nazarene University (IL)
* Orange Coast College (CA)

Pace University (NY)
* Palomar College (CA)
Pomona College (CA)
Purchase College, State University of New York

Queens College of the City University of New York
Queen's University at Kingston (ON)
Quinnipiac College (CT)

Rhode Island College
Rhode Island School of Design
Rutgers, The State University of New Jersey, Mason Gross School of the Arts
Ryerson Polytechnic University (ON)

Sacred Heart University (CT)
St. Cloud State University (MN)
Sam Houston State University (TX)
San Francisco Art Institute
San Francisco State University
San Jose State University (CA)
* Santa Barbara City College (CA)

* Santa Rosa Junior College (CA)
  Sarah Lawrence College (NY)
  School of the Art Institute of Chicago
  School of the Museum of Fine Arts (MA)
  School of Visual Arts (NY)
  Simon Fraser University (BC)
  Southern Methodist University (TX)
  State University of New York at Binghamton
  State University of New York at Buffalo
  State University of New York College at Brockport
  State University of New York College at Cortland
  State University of New York College at Fredonia
  Syracuse University (NY)

* Tallahassee Community College (FL)
  Temple University (PA)

  The Union Institute (OH)
  Université de Montréal (QB)
  University of Baltimore
  University of British Columbia
  University of California, Irvine
  University of California, Los Angeles
  University of California, San Diego
  University of California, Santa Barbara
  University of California, Santa Cruz
  University of Central Florida
  University of Chicago
  University of Colorado at Boulder
  University of Georgia
  University of Hartford (CT)
  The University of Iowa
  University of Manitoba
  University of Maryland, Baltimore County
  University of Miami (FL)
  University of Michigan
  University of Minnesota, Twin Cities Campus
  University of Nevada, Las Vegas
  University of New Mexico
  University of North Texas
  University of Pittsburgh (PA)
  University of Regina (SK)
  University of Rochester (NY)
  University of South Carolina
  University of Southern California
  University of Tennessee, Knoxville
  University of the Arts (PA)

University of the Pacific (CA)
University of Toledo (OH)
University of Toronto (ON)
University of Utah
University of Waterloo (ON)
The University of Western Ontario
University of Windsor (ON)
University of Wisconsin–Milwaukee

Vassar College (NY)

* Watkins Institute College of Art and Design (TN)
Wayne State University (MI)
Webster University (MO)
Wesleyan University (CT)
West Chester University of Pennsylvania
Wilfrid Laurier University (ON)
Wright State University (OH)

Yale University (CT)
York University (ON)

Film-Video Making/Cinematography and Production

Academy of Art College (CA)
The Advertising Arts College (CA)
Allentown College of St. Francis de Sales (PA)
American InterContinental University (CA)
American InterContinental University (GA)
American InterContinental University (United Kingdom)
American University (DC)
* Anne Arundel Community College (MD)
Antioch College (OH)
* The Art Institute of Atlanta (GA)
* The Art Institute of Fort Lauderdale (FL)
* The Art Institute of Houston (TX)
* The Art Institute of Philadelphia (PA)
* The Art Institute of Pittsburgh (PA)
* The Art Institute of Seattle (WA)
Atlanta College of Art (GA)
Bard College (NY)

Brooks Institute of Photography (CA)
Brown University (RI)
* Bucks County Community College (PA)
Burlington College (VT)

California State University, Long Beach

California State University, Northridge
Chapman University (CA)
* City College of San Francisco (CA)
City College of the City University of New York
* College of DuPage (IL)
* College of San Mateo (CA)
College of Santa Fe (NM)
* College of the Canyons (CA)
The Colorado Institute of Art
Columbia College (IL)
Columbia College–Hollywood (CA)
Concordia University (QB)
* Cumberland County College (NJ)

* Daytona Beach Community College (FL)
Drexel University (PA)

Emerson College (MA)
* Everett Community College (WA)
The Evergreen State College (WA)

Fairleigh Dickinson University, Florham-Madison Campus (NJ)
Fitchburg State College (MA)
Five Towns College (NY)
Florida Metropolitan University–Orlando College, Melbourne
Florida Metropolitan University–Orlando College, North
Florida State University
* Full Sail Real World Education (FL)

Georgia State University
Grand Valley State University (MI)

Hampshire College (MA)
* Hesser College (NH)
Hofstra University (NY)
* Holyoke Community College (MA)

* International Fine Arts College (FL)
Iowa Wesleyan College
Ithaca College (NY)

* Keiser College (FL)

* Lane Community College (OR)
* Lansing Community College (MI)
Long Island University, Southampton College, Friends World Program
    (NY)
Loyola Marymount University (CA)

Lyndon State College (VT)

Maharishi University of Management (IA)
Massachusetts College of Art
* Miami-Dade Community College (FL)
Middle Tennessee State University
Minneapolis College of Art and Design (MN)
* Minneapolis Community and Technical College (MN)
* Modesto Junior College (CA)
Montana State University–Bozeman

New York University
North Carolina School of the Arts
Northern Michigan University

Oklahoma City University
* Orange Coast College (CA)

* Pellissippi State Technical Community College (TN)
Pennsylvania State University University Park Campus
* Piedmont Community College (NC)
Point Park College (PA)
Pratt Institute (NY)

Quinnipiac College (CT)

Rochester Institute of Technology (NY)

Sacred Heart University (CT)
* Saddleback College (CA)
St. Cloud State University (MN)
* St. Louis Community College at Florissant Valley (MO)
* St. Louis Community College at Meramec (MO)
San Diego State University (CA)
Sarah Lawrence College (NY)
Savannah College of Art and Design (GA)
School of the Art Institute of Chicago
School of the Museum of Fine Arts (MA)
School of Visual Arts (NY)
* Seattle Central Community College (WA)
* Shoreline Community College (WA)
Southern California College
Southern Illinois University at Carbondale
* Southern Maine Technical College
Syracuse University (NY)

Temple University (PA)

* Union County College (NJ)
University of California, Berkeley
University of California, Santa Cruz
University of Hartford (CT)
University of Illinois at Chicago
The University of Iowa
University of Miami (FL)
University of North Carolina at Greensboro
University of Oklahoma
University of Regina (SK)
University of South Dakota
University of Southern California
University of Southern Colorado
University of the Arts (PA)
* Valencia Community College (FL)

Villa Julie College (MD)

* Waldorf College (IA)
Webster University (MO)

York University (ON)
Youngstown State University (OH)

appendix 3
Internships

Archive Films/Photos

Stock film and photographic image footage library providing historic motion picture clips and photos to advertising agencies, corporations, TV producers, news broadcasts, documentary makers, and feature films. Established in 1979. Number of employees: 130. Number of internship applications received each year: 75–100. Affiliated with The Image Bank, Dallas, Texas.

Intern Coordinator, 530 West 25th Street, New York, New York 10001. Fax: 212-645-2137.

Assistant Directors Training Program

Training program that provides 400 days of on-the-job training, supplemented by classroom seminars, in the work of second assistant directors. Established in 1965. Number of employees: 2. Number of internship applications received each year: 1,000.

Ms. Kate Tilley-Carroll, Administrator, 15260 Ventura Boulevard, Suite 1200A, Sherman Oaks, California 91403. Phone: 818-386-2545.

Association of Independent Video and Filmmakers—Foundation for Independent Video and Film

Trade association of 5,000 independent media professionals that provides advocacy and information services. Established in 1975. Number of employees: 10. Number of internship applications received each year: 40–60.

Membership Coordinator, 304 Hudson Street, 6th Floor, New York, New York 10013. Fax: 212-463-8519.

Baywatch Production Company

Television production company that produces the television show *Baywatch*. Established in 1989. Number of employees: 15. Number of internship applications received each year: 100–200.

Peter Hoffman, Internship Coordinator, 5433 Beethoven Street, Los Angeles, California 90066.

Beach Associates

Video production company that specializes in organizational communications. Established in 1979. Number of employees: 8. Number of internship applications received each year: 12–24.

Ms. Kay Leonard, 200 North Glebe Road, Suite 720, Arlington, Virginia 22203. Phone: 703-812-8813. Fax: 703-812-9710.

Buzzco Associates, Inc.

Traditional animation company with projects ranging from corporate sales films to cable network IDs to network public service announcements and national and regional commercials. Established in 1985. Number of employees: 5. Number of internship applications received each year: 10–25.

Ms. Candy Kugel, Director, Producer, 33 Bleecker Street, New York, New York 10012. Phone: 212-473-8800. Fax: 212-473-8891.

D'Elia-Wittkofski Productions

Organization that engages in production of corporate industrial videos and some broadcast videos. Established in 1981. Number of employees: 30. Number of internship applications received each year: 20–40.

Chere Tiller, Operations Coordinator, 1 Market Street, Pittsburgh, Pennsylvania 15222. Phone: 412-391-2900. Fax: 412-391-0185.

Fever Films

Film distribution and production company, focusing on experimental, independent, and short-form work. Established in 1995. Number of employees: 3. Number of internship applications received each year: 20–30.

Stephen Kent Jusick, Founder, 23 East 10th Street, #PHG, New York, New York 10003. Phone: 212-539-1023. Fax: 212-475-1399.

Film/Video Arts

Nonprofit organization that offers subsidized rates to independent film and video makers, holds classes, and provides production and postproduction equipment and services in film and video. Established in 1967. Number of employees: 15. Number of internship applications received each year: 500–1,000.

Intern Manager, 817 Broadway, New York, New York 10003. Phone: 212-673-9361. Fax: 212-475-3467.

Historic Films

Historic stock footage library specializing in archival film and musical performances. Established in 1991. Number of employees: 9. Number of internship applications received each year: 50–100.

Kevin Rice, Internship Coordinator, 12 Goodfriend Drive, East Hampton, New York 11937. Phone: 516-329-9200. Fax: 516-329-9260.

International Documentary Association

Nonprofit organization founded to promote and support the work of nonfiction and documentary film and video makers and promote international understanding through the documentary arts and sciences. Established in 1982. Number of employees: 5. Number of internship applications received each year: 50.

Ms. Grace Ouchida, Associate Director, 1551 South Robertson Boulevard, Suite 201, Los Angeles, California 90035-4257. Fax: 310-785-9334.

International Video Services

Videotape duplication and editing facility. Established in 1980. Number of employees: 10. Number of internship applications received each year: 10–20.

Alexander Shahgholi, President, 1501 Broadway, Suite 515, New York, New York 10036. Phone: 212-730-1411. Fax: 212-730-5217.

Jazbo Productions

Feature film, television, and live stage production company involved in the development of feature films and made-for-television productions for the networks and major studios. Established in 1985. Number of employees: 1. Number of internship applications received each year: 150–200.

Ms. Jill Marti, President, 185 Pier Avenue, Santa Monica, California 90405. Phone: 310-664-6004. Fax: 310-664-3656.

LeFrak Productions, Inc.

Film and television development company headed by an independent producer. Established in 1980. Number of employees: 5. Number of internship applications received each year: 50–100.

Internship Coordinator, 40 West 57th Street, Suite 409, New York, New York 10019. Phone: 212-541-9444. Fax: 212-974-8205.

Lighthouse Productions

Feature film and television production company. Established in 1974. Number of employees: 2. Number of internship applications received each year: 150–400.

Internship Coordinator, 120 El Camino Drive, Suite 212, Beverly Hills, California 90212.

Lovett Productions, Inc.

Independent production company that produces documentary and reality programming, video news releases, industrials, and independent films. Established in 1989. Number of employees: 5. Number of internship applications received each year: 100.

Rebecca Levi, Office Manager, 155 Sixth Avenue, 10th Floor, New York, New York 10013. Phone: 212-242-8999. Fax: 212-242-7347.

Lucasfilm, Ltd.

Lucasfilm provides business services for productions by Lucasfilm. Established in 1971. Number of employees: 200. Number of internship applications received each year: 200–500.

Amy Baur, Employment Manager and Program Specialist, Box 2009, San Rafael, California 94912. Fax: 415-662-2460.

Magnum Photos, Inc.

Cooperative photo agency with active editorial, archive, corporate, and advertising departments; archive contains over 1 million pictures representing 55 photographers. Established in 1947. Number of employees: 18. Number of internship applications received each year: 250–300.

Jan Mun, Intern Program Manager, 151 West 25th Street, 5th Floor, New York, New York 10001. Phone: 212-929-6000. Fax: 212-929-9325.

Mary Perillo, Inc.

Company that produces film and video products, including video art, music and dance performances, music videos, commercials, Sesame Street shorts, and high-end graphics. Established in 1983. Number of employees: 2. Number of internship applications received each year: 150–200.

Ms. Molly Maguire, 125 Cedar Street, #8 South, New York, New York 10006. Phone: 212-608-3943.

Maryland Film Office

State organization marketing Maryland's film/video industry and locations to the motion picture and television production industry. Established in 1980. Number of employees: 5. Number of internship applications received each year: 80–150. Affiliated with the Maryland Department of Business and Economic Development, Baltimore, Maryland.

Mr. Michael B. Styer, Director, 217 East Redwood Street, 9th Floor, Baltimore, Maryland 21202. Phone: 410-767-6340. Fax: 410-333-0044.

MD Wax/Courier Films

Distributor of foreign and independent films. Established in 1983. Number of employees: 2. Number of internship applications received each year: 50–75. Affiliated with Morton Dennis Wax, New York, New York.

Ms. Sandra Wax, 1560 Broadway, Room 706, New York, New York 10036. Fax: 212-302-5364.

Metro-Goldwyn-Mayer/United Artists

Movie company that releases first-run films into the domestic market. Established in 1924. Number of employees: 7. Number of internship applications received each year: 50–150.

Lisa Zaks, Internship Coordinator, 1350 Sixth Avenue, 24th Floor, New York, New York 10019. Phone: 212-708-0372. Fax: 212-708-0370.

National Association of College Broadcasters

Association that provides support services to student broadcast stations. Established in 1988. Number of employees: 3. Number of internship applications received each year: 50–75.

Laura Nein, Internship Coordinator, Brown University, Box 1824, Providence, Rhode Island 02912-1824. Fax: 401-863-2221.

Northwest Film Center

Regional media arts center serving the Northwest with film and video exhibitions, continuing education, artist-in-the-schools programs, and fellowship programs. Established in 1972. Number of employees: 15. Number of internship applications received each year: 30–60. Affiliated with the Portland Art Museum, Portland, Oregon.

Internship Coordinator, 1219 Southwest Park Avenue, Portland, Oregon 97205. Phone: 503-221-1156. Fax: 503-294-0874.

Open City Films

Independent film production company. Established in 1993. Number of employees: 5. Number of internship applications received each year: 100–200.

Ben Bohen, 198 Avenue of the Americas, New York, New York 10013. Fax: 212-343-1849.

Partos Company

Talent and literary agency representing both film and commercial clients, including directors, writers, directors of photography, and editors. Established in 1991. Number of employees: 3. Number of internship applications received each year: 100–300.

Internship Coordinator, 6363 Wilshire Boulevard, Suite 227, Los Angeles, California 90048. Phone: 213-876-5500.

Polygram/A&M Records

Record label company in the music industry. Established in 1966. Number of employees: 290. Number of internship applications received each year: 150–200.

Patty Mitchell, Manager, Human Resources, 1416 North LaBrea Avenue, Hollywood, California 90028. Phone: 310-385-4111. Fax: 213-856-2798.

Public Interest Video Network

Media center producing public television documentaries and assisting issue-oriented nonprofit organizations and the government in using the media. Established in 1979. Number of employees: 4–5. Number of internship applications received each year: 30–40.

Ms. Elsa D. Newman, Assistant Director/Attorney, 4704 Overbrook Road, Bethesda, Maryland 20816. Phone: 301-656-7244.

S.O.S. Productions, Inc.

Film, audio, video, and postproduction facility making television commercials and training videos. Established in 1981. Number of employees: 44. Number of internship applications received each year: 50–75.

Cory Wills, Production Manager, 753 Harmon Avenue, Columbus, Ohio 43223. Fax: 614-221-3836.

Simon & Goodman Picture Company

Documentary film company.

Beth Westrate, Associate Producer, 2095 Broadway, Suite 402, New York, New York 10023. Fax: 212-721-0922.

Stone vs. Stone

Film production for studios (independent and cable), with an emphasis on nonfiction-based political thriller material and other book projects. Number of internship applications received each year: 50–100.

Web Stone, 189 Franklin Street, 3rd Floor, New York, New York 10013. Phone: 212-941-1200.

Unitel Video

Organization that provides interactive multimedia services and development and support for educational, marketing, training, exhibit, promotion, archival, business presentation applications, animation, video production, and audio services. Established in 1973. Number of employees: 35. Number of internship applications received each year: 15–20. Affiliated with Unitel, New York, New York.

Michael McCall, Executive Producer, 8 West 38th Street, 2nd Floor, New York, New York 10018.

Women Make Movies, Inc.

National women's media organization that facilitates the production, promotion, and distribution of films and videotapes by and about women. Established in 1972. Number of employees: 10. Number of internship applications received each year: 60–75.

Krista Anderson, Internship Coordinator, 462 Broadway, 5th Floor, New York, New York 10013. Fax: 212-925-2052.

Index

NOTES

A LIFETIME OF LEARNING AWAITS YOU IN EVERY PETERSON'S GUIDE

Finding the right job is never easy. Peterson's on line at the Career & Education Center at petersons.com gives you the tools and the help you need to find and win the job of your dreams.

At **petersons.com** you can
- Search for career opportunities
- Find helpful articles to steer your search
- Get advice on building a portfolio

And if you're looking for advice on finding the right graduate program, look no further than the **Enrollment Message Center** at **petersons.com**!
- Explore program options by discipline
- E-mail program contacts for more information
- Best of all? It's **FREE**

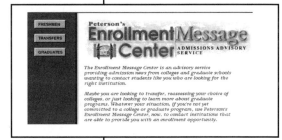

Let Peterson's be your online guide to the future!

PETERSON'S
Princeton, New Jersey
www.petersons.com

1-800-338-3282

Wait! There's more!➜